Israel: our Christian Heritage
Israel: our Christian Destiny

by

Chris A. Legebow

Copyright © 2019 Chris A. Legebow

All rights reserved.

ISBN: 978-1-988914-12-1

DEDICATION

I dedicate this book to all Christian and Messianic ministries and who have presented teaching concerning Israel , because of them, I know the importance of Israel and Jewish people to God and all Christians.

I pray for the peace and prosperity of Jerusalem and all of Israel and all Jewish people. May they all come to know Jesus as Messiah.

Israel our Christian Heritage: Israel our Christian Destiny

CONTENTS

	Acknowledgments	i
1	God Chose Israel	3
2	Abraham	10
3	After Joseph	30
4	Moses	34
5	Mosaic Covenant	52
6	Kings of Israel	62
7	David Becomes King	66
8	Destruction of the Temple	84
9	Daniel	86

CONTENTS

10	The Rebuilding of the Temple	94
11	Book of Hosea	103
12	Malachi	112
13	God's Special Mercy on Israel	114
14	Jesus the Messiah	117
15	Jesus is the Living Word of God	122
16	The Third Temple	130
17	The 2nd Coming of Christ	146
18	New Heavens and New Earth: New Jerusalem	166
19	Conclusion	170
20	Epilogue	174

ACKNOWLEDGMENTS

All scripture taken from BibleGateway.com
MEV
KJV

Israel images from google images

INTRODUCTION

Israel is a small but mighty country. The people there live a free and peaceful life. Yet they are receiving attacks of missiles by the neighbouring countries who hate her existence. The Israeli army has a significant purpose – they defend Israel. Israel is not fighting against anyone. Israel as a nation defends herself from enemy attacks. As Prime minister Netanyahu has stated "If the other nations stopped fighting against Israel, there would be no war. If Israel stopped fighting to defend Israel, there would be no Israel."

Those surrounding fighting nations hate Israel so much they would try to destroy her to possess her land. The root of antisemitism can be found in the scriptures. The root of the hatred can be found in the Scriptures. God chose Israel. God's covenant is with Israel. God's blessing is on Israel. All scripture is from Israel. All our Biblical prophets and apostles are from Israel. Our Saviour is from Israel. Israel is our Christian heritage. We should care for Israel. We should pray for Israel and we should oppose all antisemitism. Christians should align with Israel.

Satan, an angel who was cast out of God's presence hates God and deceived Eve and compelled Adam to sin against God. The root of hatred against God's people is the devil. Throughout the scriptures there have been attacks on Israel, but God has always protected her.

Jesus Christ will return to the Mount of Olives in Jerusalem and Christian believers will rule with him there for a thousand years. Many Jews shall come to Jesus Messiah as Christ appears on earth once more to fulfill the prayer of the Apostle Paul "all of Israel shall be saved" (Romans 11:25) As Christians, our destiny is with Israel.

My book is a scriptural study of the importance of Israel to us as Christians. Our destiny is the same. Jews and Gentiles shall become one in Messiah Jesus (Gal 3: 28). We should pray for Israel, give financially, purchase Israeli and align with others who honour Israel. It is my hope that through this book you will recognize the God is Israel is our God: the destiny of Israel is our destiny.

CHAPTER 1 GOD CHOSE ISRAEL

The start of Israel is the creation of Adam and Eve. God chose to create people so that he could speak with us and we could be in relationship with Him. Human origin is the origin of Israel because God is the God of Israel. God created the earth and all of the universes. God created all things, all scientific aspects of systems and physical properties. He created all types of animals and the land and oceans of the earth.

God created all

Genesis 1: [31] God saw all that he had made, and it was very good. And there was evening, and there was morning—the sixth day.

God created Adam and Eve. His desire was to create us to be his family. We are His people and He is our God. He created us for His pleasure. He created woman from the man because Adam did not have any creature to be his mate. All animals were male and female. God created Adam and Eve – male and female. It was so they could populate the earth but also for companionship.

Revelation 4: [11] "You are worthy, our Lord and God, to receive glory and honor and power, for you created all things,

and by your will they were created
and have their being."

God created Adam and Eve

Genesis 2: [8] Now the LORD God had planted a garden in the east, in Eden; and there he put the man he had formed. [9] The LORD God made all kinds of trees grow out of the ground—trees that were pleasing to the eye and good for food. In the middle of the garden were the tree of life and the tree of the knowledge of good and evil.

Genesis 2: [21] So the LORD God caused the man to fall into a deep sleep; and while he was sleeping, he took one of the man's ribs[g] and then closed up the place with flesh. [22] Then the LORD God made a woman from the rib[h] he had taken out of the man, and he brought her to the man.

Adam and Eve could have lived in the garden at Eden all their lives with joy and no sorrow or pain. Because they directly disobeyed God's commandment not to eat of the tree of good and evil, sin entered the world. They were cast out of the garden of Eden and had to toil and suffer with thorns and thistles and the consequences of sin.

Genesis 3: [14] So the LORD God said to the serpent, "Because you have done this,

"Cursed are you above all livestock
   and all wild animals!
You will crawl on your belly
   and you will eat dust
   all the days of your life.
[15] And I will put enmity
   between you and the woman,
   and between your offspring[a] and hers;
he will crush[b] your head,
   and you will strike his heel."
[16] To the woman he said,

"I will make your pains in childbearing very severe;
   with painful labor you will give birth to children.
Your desire will be for your husband,
   and he will rule over you."
[17] To Adam he said, "Because you listened to your wife and ate fruit from the tree about which I commanded you, 'You must not eat from it,'

"Cursed is the ground because of you;
   through painful toil you will eat food from it
   all the days of your life.
[18] It will produce thorns and thistles for you,
   and you will eat the plants of the field.

¹⁹ By the sweat of your brow
   you will eat your food
until you return to the ground,
   since from it you were taken;
for dust you are
   and to dust you will return."
²⁰ Adam[c] named his wife Eve,[d] because she would become the mother of all the living.

²¹ The LORD God made garments of skin for Adam and his wife and clothed them. ²² And the LORD God said, "The man has now become like one of us, knowing good and evil. He must not be allowed to reach out his hand and take also from the tree of life and eat, and live forever." ²³ So the LORD God banished him from the Garden of Eden to work the ground from which he had been taken. ²⁴ After he drove the man out, he placed on the east side[e] of the Garden of Eden cherubim and a flaming sword flashing back and forth to guard the way to the tree of life.

The sin of Adam impacted all the earth, all creatures of the earth and all people of the earth – continuing to this day. Because sin entered the world, the children of Adam and Eve (and all people born on the earth afterwards) fought and Cain killed Abel because of jealousy and strife. The people of the earth were not serving their creator or worshipping God. They were indulging in dins of the flesh and there was fighting and violence in the earth. It was so much that God regretted creating people.

Genesis 6: ⁵The LORD saw how great the wickedness of the human race had become on the earth, and that every inclination of the thoughts of the human heart was only evil all the time. ⁶The LORD regretted that he had made human beings on the earth, and his heart was deeply troubled. ⁷So the LORD said, "I will wipe from the face of the earth the human race I have created—and with them the animals, the birds and the creatures that move along the ground—for I regret that I have made them." ⁸But Noah found favor in the eyes of the LORD.

Noah was a true believer in God, and he obeyed God as God spoke with him. God instructed him to build an ark (a huge boat) so that some of all the animals and the people who would repent could be saved from the flood that God was going to send to end the wickedness of the people. It was a judgment on the people, but it would affect all the earth and all the animals. Man's sin affects all within his sphere of authority.

Genesis 6: [12] God saw how corrupt the earth had become, for all the people on earth had corrupted their ways. [13] So God said to Noah, "I am going to put an end to all people, for the earth is filled with violence because of them. I am surely going to destroy both them and the earth. [14] So make yourself an ark of cypress[c] wood; make rooms in it and coat it with pitch inside and out. [15] This is how you are to build it: The ark is to be three hundred cubits long, fifty cubits wide and thirty cubits high.[d] [16] Make a roof for it, leaving below the roof an opening one cubit[e] high all around.[f] Put a door in the side of the ark and make lower, middle and upper decks. [17] I am going to bring floodwaters on the earth to destroy all life under the heavens, every creature that has the breath of life in it. Everything on earth will perish. [18] But I will establish my covenant with you, and you will enter the ark—you and your sons and your wife and your sons' wives with you. [19] You are to bring into the ark two of all living creatures, male and female, to keep them alive with you. [20] Two of every kind of bird, of every kind of animal and of every kind of creature that moves along the ground will come to you to be kept alive. [21] You are to take every kind of food that is to be eaten and store it away as food for you and for them."

²²Noah did everything just as God commanded him.

For 120 years Noah preached to the people around him who wanted to know what he was building and why. (2 Peter 2). Only Noah's family believed him; they and the animals went into the ark and were spared. It rained; it had never rained until that day. The flood covered all of the earth for more than 40 days. Life began new with Noah and his family and the animals. Noah built an altar to God praising Him for their salvation (Genesis 8).

All the descendants of Noah were not believers because although the wicked people were destroyed, there was sin the sin of Adam- even in Noah's family. The earth became filled with people over the years and the next person God revealed Himself to was Abraham. Abraham was an idol worshipper in the land of Ur. His family was in the business of creating idols. God spoke to Abraham sovereignly. God chose him. God spoke to him and Abraham obeyed God.

2 ABRAHAM

Abraham

Abraham lived in Ur of the Chaldees; they were idol worshippers. God chose Abraham spoke with him – promised to make of him a people. Abraham obeyed God and God made special promises to him that he would be the start of a great nation. He promised that his descendants would cover the earth. God's blessing was on Abraham's life.

Gen 12:1 **The LORD had said to Abram, "Go from your country, your people and your father's household to the land I will show you.**

[2] **"I will make you into a great nation,**
   and I will bless you;
I will make your name great,
   and you will be a blessing.[a]
[3] **I will bless those who bless you,**
   and whoever curses you I will curse;
and all peoples on earth
   will be blessed through you."[b]

₄So Abram went, as the LORD had told him; and Lot went with him. Abram was seventy-five years old when he set out from Harran. ₅He took his wife Sarai, his nephew Lot, all the possessions they had accumulated and the people they had acquired in Harran, and they set out for the land of Canaan, and they arrived there.

To obey God and leave all his family and his dwelling to go to a place he did not know of, took faith. Abraham believed God. That is why he is mentioned in the book of Hebrews 11 as a hero of faith. Although they did not know the place – they believed God would direct them to the place of promised. It became known as the promised land – it was to become the nation of Israel.

Gen 13: ₁₄The LORD said to Abram after Lot had parted from him, "Look around from where you are, to the north and south, to the east and west. ₁₅All the land that you see I will give to you and your offspring[a] forever. ₁₆I will make your offspring like the dust of the earth, so that if anyone could count the dust, then your offspring could be counted. ₁₇Go, walk through the length and breadth of the land, for I am giving it to you."

The land was Canaan. It was to become Israel. That piece of land was to become a priority to all the others in Scripture. A single place was to determine the children of Abraham and all his descendants of promise. It became a place people would fight over for generations. God promised it to Abraham and his descendants. It is start of God's covenant with Israel. God began promising to Abraham special blessings that apply to Israel. Abraham's part of the covenant was to obey God and to circumcise all males.

Abraham's son was born when he was almost 100 years old. His wife was nearly the same age and past her age of child bearing. God sent angels to speak with Abraham; they were disguised as men. They gave a prophetic word that Sarah would give birth. She did. The child was the child of promise – Isaac. Although Abraham many other children – God chose Isaac to inherit the land. Abraham obeyed God and released his blessings upon Isaac. The blessing or covenant with Abraham continued with Isaac. Abraham would not let his son marry just anyone. He told him to get his wife from among their relatives.

Isaac

Genesis 26: ²The LORD appeared to Isaac and said, "Do not go down to Egypt; live in the land where I tell you to live. ³Stay in this land for a while, and I will be with you and will bless you. For to you and your descendants I will give all these lands and will confirm the oath I swore to your father Abraham. ⁴ I will make your descendants as numerous as the stars in the sky and will give them all these lands, and through your offspring[a] all nations on earth will be blessed,[b] ⁵ because Abraham obeyed me and did everything I required of him, keeping my commands, my decrees and my instructions." ⁶ So Isaac stayed in Gerar.

God promised as many inheritances as grains of sand – as many as stars in sky (Gen 26: 24). It was not physically possible, but God did what He promised. The result is all of Israel and all Semitic peoples.

(Genesis 21: 4) Circumcision was an outward sign of cutting away of flesh. It was symbolic of total commitment to God. Circumcision takes on new meaning and is essential in Christianity and in Judaism as an inward circumcision of heart so people can love God truly. It means the sin nature has been cut out of the heart and people can live wholly unto God.

Romans 2: ²⁸ A person is not a Jew who is one only outwardly, nor is circumcision merely outward and physical. ²⁹ No, a person is a Jew who is one inwardly; and circumcision is circumcision of the heart, by the Spirit, not by the written code. Such a person's praise is not from other people, but from God.

God spoke with Abraham and shared the future of Abraham's people with him 400 years of slavery Genesis 15: 13 as well as the deliver who would come. Isaac received the blessing and lived pleasing to God in relationship with God. After the death of his mother, he married.

Isaac's wife gave birth to twins: Esau and Jacob. Though Jacob had a deceptive nature and stole his elder brother's birthright, stole the elder brother's blessing by deceiving Isaac, he was the person God chose to pass the blessing to. Jacob deceived the almost blind Isaac by pretending to be his brother Esau. He disguised himself as his brother, to deceive Isaac in giving him the blessing rather than let the blessing go to the elder son; he heated Esau of his chance of a first fruit blessing.

Genesis 27: [22] Jacob went close to his father Isaac, who touched him and said, "The voice is the voice of Jacob, but the hands are the hands of Esau." [23] He did not recognize him, for his hands were hairy like those of his brother Esau; so he proceeded to bless him. [24] "Are you really my son Esau?" he asked.

"I am," he replied.

²⁵ Then he said, "My son, bring me some of your game to eat, so that I may give you my blessing."

Jacob brought it to him and he ate; and he brought some wine and he drank. ²⁶ Then his father Isaac said to him, "Come here, my son, and kiss me."

²⁷ So he went to him and kissed him. When Isaac caught the smell of his clothes, he blessed him and said,

"Ah, the smell of my son
   is like the smell of a field
   that the LORD has blessed.
²⁸ May God give you heaven's dew
   and earth's richness—
   an abundance of grain and new wine.
²⁹ May nations serve you
   and peoples bow down to you.
Be lord over your brothers,
   and may the sons of your mother bow down to you.
May those who curse you be cursed
   and those who bless you be blessed."

    Despite Jacob's deceptive nature, God chose him to impart a blessing and honoured the blessings of Isaac on him. Jacob had a dual nature. He was gentle and kind but deceptive. Jacob feared for his life because Esau was angry and violent. Jacob escaped to his uncle Laban who was a deceiver and lived there and worked for him as a shepherd. God chose Jacob – Jacob married both daughters of Laban because Laban deceived him and gave his elder daughter in disguise. Jacob truly loved Rachel. Because of the deception, he worked 7 more years to marry Rachel. Laban was a deceiver, so Jacob experienced his match. He finally got the courage to move his large family of two wives and children and flocks and herds away from Laban. He knew he could not stay with him. God spoke to him.

Genesis 31: ³Then the LORD said to Jacob, "Go back to the land of your fathers and to your relatives, and I will be with you."

Jacob obeyed. Laban went after him because Jacob was a good servant to him, and both his daughters and all his grandchildren were with him. God spoke to Laban warning him.

Genesis 31: ²²On the third day Laban was told that Jacob had fled. ²³Taking his relatives with him, he pursued Jacob for seven days and caught up with him in the hill country of Gilead. ²⁴Then God came to Laban the Aramean in a dream at night and said to him, "Be careful not to say anything to Jacob, either good or bad."

Laban was angry because one of his idols was missing. He accused Jacob of stealing it. Jacob had no knowledge it, but Rachel did. She took it and hid it from everyone. Jacob made it clear to Laban that he wanted to live on his own. Laban and Jacob made a peace agreement.

Jacob encountered God and it changed his life as well as his name. The place was called Peniel. Jacob the deceiver was changed by God who encountered him, in the form of an angel, blessed him, prospered him and spoke with him because of promises to Abraham. Jacob was changed because he was inwardly changed; he no longer was deceptive – he was wholly living for God. God changed Jacob's name to Israel. Through his wives and concubines, he had 12 sons: the origin of the 12 tribes of Israel. They are the tribes that populated all the land of Canaan - the land that God promised to Abraham.

Jacob made his decision to go out of Laban's dwelling. God wrestled with an angel. It is symbolic of his dying to his old nature and new desire to serve God. He was never the same after it. He wholly served God and imparted to his children the things he learned from Isaac.

Genesis 32: [22] That night Jacob got up and took his two wives, his two female servants and his eleven sons and crossed the ford of the Jabbok. [23] After he had sent them across the stream, he sent over all his possessions. ²⁴ So Jacob was left alone, and a man wrestled with him till daybreak. ²⁵ When the man saw that he could not overpower him, he touched the socket of Jacob's hip so that his hip was wrenched as he wrestled with the man. ²⁶ Then the man said, "Let me go, for it is daybreak."

But Jacob replied, "I will not let you go unless you bless me."

²⁷ The man asked him, "What is your name?"

"Jacob," he answered.

²⁸ Then the man said, "Your name will no longer be Jacob, but Israel,[f] because you have struggled with God and with humans and have overcome."

²⁹ Jacob said, "Please tell me your name."

But he replied, "Why do you ask my name?" Then he blessed him there.

³⁰ So Jacob called the place Peniel,[g] saying, "It is because I saw God face to face, and yet my life was spared."

God blessed Leah the first wife of Jacob now called Israel with many children. Rachel did not give birth until later. She was the wife he loved most. She gave birth also to Joseph. She died in childbirth or her son Benjamin. Israel had 12 sons who all had different characteristics. Some served God. Some had a dual nature of serving God but sinning also. These 12 sons are the foundations of the 12 tribes of the nation of Israel. God chose these sons to inherit the blessing and to populate the promised land of Israel. They dwelt in the land of Canaan until there was a horrible famine. These are the 12 sons of Jacob (Genesis 35):

[23] The sons of Leah:

Reuben the firstborn of Jacob,

Simeon, Levi, Judah, Issachar and Zebulun.

[24] The sons of Rachel:

Joseph and Benjamin.

[25] The sons of Rachel's servant Bilhah:

Dan and Naphtali.

[26] The sons of Leah's servant Zilpah:

Gad and Asher.

Joseph

The elder brothers hated Joseph because he was their father's favourite son. Jacob also loved Rachel more than Leah. Joseph was given special gifts and special responsibility even though he was the youngest shepherd. Their hatred of him was so strong they threw him in a deep pit and would have left him there to die. One of his brothers thought to profit from the situation by selling him.

Genesis 37:²⁶ Judah said to his brothers, "What will we gain if we kill our brother and cover up his blood? ²⁷ Come, let's sell him to the Ishmaelites and not lay our hands on him; after all, he is our brother, our own flesh and blood." His brothers agreed.

Joseph was the youngest – the favourite – now suddenly become a slave in Egypt. God had spoken to Joseph in dreams and revealed things to him that would all come true. Joseph did not have wisdom and shared his dreams with his brothers, and it sounded as though he was bragging. His brothers were not spiritual – they were carnal. They didn't believe his dreams. They did not show respect towards Jacob or Joseph because Jacob loved Joseph more. God had mercy on Joseph and a special blessing was on his life so that whatever he did he prospered. Even as a slave in Egypt, he prospered. He was raised to a position of authority in his master's home. The blessing of God was upon him.

Genesis 39: ² The LORD was with Joseph so that he prospered, and he lived in the house of his Egyptian master. ³ When his master saw that the LORD was with him and that the LORD gave him success in everything he did, ⁴ Joseph found favor in his eyes and became his attendant. Potiphar put him in charge of his household, and he entrusted to his care everything he owned. ⁵From the time he put him in charge of his household and of all that he owned, the LORD blessed the household of the Egyptian because of Joseph. The blessing of the LORD was on everything Potiphar had, both in the house and in the field. ⁶So Potiphar left everything he had in Joseph's care; with Joseph in charge, he did not concern himself with anything except the food he ate.

Joseph was so excellent, handsome and talented and skillful. He was an excellent servant entrusted with much, but a terrible thing happened to him. Potiphar's wife kept lusting after him and threw herself at him. He escaped but she was so much forcing herself on him, she took his robe from his body. He escaped not wanted to sin against God or his master. Because of the false accusation, from a person in authority – Joseph was thrown into prison.

While he was in prison, he gained favour with the guards and was made an overseer in the prison. He organized things and they ran smoothly. God's blessing was on Joseph even though his circumstance was not anywhere near like the dreams God had given him. While he was in prison both the king's baker and cupbearer were thrown into prison by the Pharaoh because they were accused of stealing from Pharaoh. They both, had unusual dreams that they shared with Joseph. God gave Joseph the interpretation of the dreams.

Genesis 40: ⁹ So the chief cupbearer told Joseph his dream. He said to him, "In my dream I saw a vine in front of me, ¹⁰ and on the vine were three branches. As soon as it budded, it blossomed, and its clusters ripened into grapes. ¹¹ Pharaoh's cup was in my hand, and I took the grapes, squeezed them into Pharaoh's cup and put the cup in his hand."

Joseph prophetically interpreted the dream. He appealed to the cup bearer to have mercy on him and remember him so that he might get out of prison.

¹² "This is what it means," Joseph said to him. "The three branches are three days. ¹³ Within three days Pharaoh will lift up your head and restore you to your position, and you will put Pharaoh's cup in his hand, just as you used to do when you were his cupbearer. ¹⁴ But when all goes well with you, remember me and show me kindness; mention me to Pharaoh and get me out of this prison. ¹⁵ I was forcibly carried off from the land of the Hebrews, and even here I have done nothing to deserve being put in a dungeon."

Genesis 40: [16] When the chief baker saw that Joseph had given a favorable interpretation, he said to Joseph, "I too had a dream: On my head were three baskets of bread.[a] [17] In the top basket were all kinds of baked goods for Pharaoh, but the birds were eating them out of the basket on my head."

Joseph interpreted his dream also, but the results were not changed from the truth even though it meant the baker would die.

[18] "This is what it means," Joseph said. "The three baskets are three days. [19] Within three days Pharaoh will lift off your head and impale your body on a pole. And the birds will eat away your flesh."

The prophetic interpretation of both dreams came true, but the cupbearer did not remember Joseph.

Genesis 40: [23] The chief cupbearer, however, did not remember Joseph; he forgot him.

One night, Pharaoh had a dream that bothered him so much he called for the magicians and soothsayers to come interpret the dream, but they could not.

Genesis 41: [8] In the morning his mind was troubled, so he sent for all the magicians and wise men of Egypt. Pharaoh told them his dreams, but no one could interpret them for him.

Suddenly the cupbearer remembered Joseph.

⁹Then the chief cupbearer said to Pharaoh, "Today I am reminded of my shortcomings. ¹⁰Pharaoh was once angry with his servants, and he imprisoned me and the chief baker in the house of the captain of the guard. ¹¹Each of us had a dream the same night, and each dream had a meaning of its own. ¹²Now a young Hebrew was there with us, a servant of the captain of the guard. We told him our dreams, and he interpreted them for us, giving each man the interpretation of his dream. ¹³And things turned out exactly as he interpreted them to us: I was restored to my position, and the other man was impaled."

Because the cupbearer remembered Joseph, Joseph was taken out of prison to speak with the Pharaoh concerning the dreams. Pharaoh told his dreams to Joseph and God gave Joseph the interpretation. Joseph gave the glory to God.

Genesis 41: ²⁵Then Joseph said to Pharaoh, "The dreams of Pharaoh are one and the same. God has revealed to Pharaoh what he is about to do. ²⁶The seven good cows are seven years, and the seven good heads of grain are seven years; it is one and the same dream. ²⁷The seven lean, ugly cows that came up afterward are seven years, and so are the seven worthless heads of grain scorched by the east wind: They are seven years of famine.

²⁸ "It is just as I said to Pharaoh: God has shown Pharaoh what he is about to do. ²⁹ Seven years of great abundance are coming throughout the land of Egypt, ³⁰ but seven years of famine will follow them. Then all the abundance in Egypt will be forgotten, and the famine will ravage the land. ³¹ The abundance in the land will not be remembered, because the famine that follows it will be so severe. ³² The reason the dream was given to Pharaoh in two forms is that the matter has been firmly decided by God, and God will do it soon.

³³ "And now let Pharaoh look for a discerning and wise man and put him in charge of the land of Egypt. ³⁴ Let Pharaoh appoint commissioners over the land to take a fifth of the harvest of Egypt during the seven years of abundance. ³⁵ They should collect all the food of these good years that are coming and store up the grain under the authority of Pharaoh, to be kept in the cities for food. ³⁶ This food should be held in reserve for the country, to be used during the seven years of famine that will come upon Egypt, so that the country may not be ruined by the famine."

God gave Joseph the interpretation; he also gave him favour with Pharaoh. Pharaoh gave Joseph authority beyond what anyone could imagine. It was God's favour on him; although he was a slave – suddenly the same day he was presented to the highest ruler in Egypt. His life of consistent serving, honouring God kept the blessing of God on his life. He was promoted to a position higher than any ordinary Egyptian could obtain. He had authority in Egypt only second to Pharaoh himself. God used an Israelite to preserve and protect the nation of Egypt; because of it, God protected and kept the nation of Israel.

Genesis 41: ³⁹ Then Pharaoh said to Joseph, "Since God has made all this known to you, there is no one so discerning and wise as you. ⁴⁰ You shall be in charge of my palace, and all my people are to submit to your orders. Only with respect to the throne will I be greater than you."

Joseph was promoted to a high position in Egypt because of the dream interpretation – but it was really because the favour of God was on him. The special blessing upon him was the same blessing God had given to Abraham and Isaac. It is the covenant blessing of Abraham; God's covenants are eternal. All of Joseph's dreams of being raised to a high position of authority all came true. While he stored grain and stuff for the 7 years of plenty, he prepared for the famine that would follow.

The famine started and Joseph's family came to Egypt to buy wheat because there was no other way to get it. Joseph recognized them and did not immediately reveal himself to them. He did reveal himself once all the brothers came and he instructed them to bring Israel to live in the land of Goshen to spare their families' lives. They did. This leaving of the land of promise was temporary but necessary. All of Joseph's life, the Israelites prospered in Goshen. Their flocks and herds were disgusting to the Egyptians, so the closest they could get to Egypt was Goshen. This also allowed them to worship the true God of Israel rather than the pagan gods of Egypt. Israel blessed his 12 sons with spiritual blessings. Gen 49: 2-28. The blessings were appropriate to each son – different depending on their character.

The death of Jacob/ Israel

Jacob realized the importance of the promises of God and his keeping of them. He knew that God's promise to Abraham was important to all his children and those who would follow. He prayed a blessing on each one of them. He knew he should be buried in the land of promise. He realized the stay in Egypt was temporary and that God would create a nation after him in Canaan.

Genesis 49: [29] Then he gave them these instructions: "I am about to be gathered to my people. Bury me with my fathers in the cave in the field of Ephron the Hittite, [30] the cave in the field of Machpelah, near Mamre in Canaan, which Abraham bought along with the field as a burial place from Ephron the Hittite. ³¹ There Abraham and his wife Sarah were buried, there Isaac and his wife Rebekah were buried, and there I buried Leah. ³² The field and the cave in it were bought from the Hittites.[D]"

³³ When Jacob had finished giving instructions to his sons, he drew his feet up into the bed, breathed his last and was gathered to his people.

    God shared future of Israel with Abraham – warning him prophetically that his descendants they would be slaves for 400 years in Egypt. After the death of Joseph, there was prosperity in Goshen until an Egyptian ruler got into authority that did not know Joseph or respect him or what he had done to save all of Egypt.

3 AFTER JOSEPH

Life for the Israelites had been good. They prospered and flourished so much so that they were numerous and strong. They were not in the promised land of Canaan though; they were in Goshen. None of them made any move towards going back to the land they came from because life in Egypt was good for them. Part of the blessing on Abraham meant they must inherit and dwell in the promised land of Israel. A day came when there arose rulers in Egypt who did not know Joseph and they were carnal and feared the number of Israelites living so close to them.

Exodus 1: [6] Now Joseph and all his brothers and all that generation died, [7] but the Israelites were exceedingly fruitful; they multiplied greatly, increased in numbers and became so numerous that the land was filled with them.
[8] Then a new king, to whom Joseph meant nothing, came to power in Egypt. [9] "Look," he said to his people, "the Israelites have become far too numerous for us. [10] Come, we must deal shrewdly with them or they will become even more numerous and, if war breaks out, will join our enemies, fight against us and leave the country."

[11] So they put slave masters over them to oppress them with forced labor, and they built Pithom and

Rameses as store cities for Pharaoh. [12] But the more they were oppressed, the more they multiplied and spread; so the Egyptians came to dread the Israelites [13] and worked them ruthlessly. [14] They made their lives bitter with harsh labor in brick and mortar and with all kinds of work in the fields; in all their harsh labor the Egyptians worked them ruthlessly.

Israel prospered but suddenly became slaves to the Egyptians because of the ruler's jealousy of the blessing on Israel and the fear they would attack Egypt. Their abuse was severe and horrible, but the Israelites still worshipped God and prayed for a deliverer. They believed a deliverer would arise and bring them freedom. During 400 years of slavery Israel served in Egypt. The people had become part of Egypt. They were no longer the distinct people that first entered Egypt with Joseph's protection. They believed in God but became accustomed to the leeks, the onions, the garlic, the special things of Egypt. Some of them were not wholly serving God. God promised a deliver would arise and it so bothered the Egyptians that they feared it could be true, so they ordered the death of the first sons of the Israelites. The Egyptian midwives knew it was wrong to murder children and they lied to save them.

Exodus 1: [15] The king of Egypt said to the Hebrew midwives, whose names were Shiphrah and Puah, [16] "When you are helping the Hebrew women during childbirth on the delivery stool, if you see that the baby is a boy, kill him; but if it is a girl, let her live." [17] The midwives, however, feared God and did not do what the king of Egypt had told them to do; they let the boys live. [18] Then the king of Egypt summoned the midwives and asked them, "Why have you done this? Why have you let the boys live?"

[19] The midwives answered Pharaoh, "Hebrew women are not like Egyptian women; they are vigorous and give birth before the midwives arrive."

[20] So God was kind to the midwives and the people increased and became even more numerous. [21] And because the midwives feared God, he gave them families of their own.

Israel our Christian Heritage: Israel our Christian Destiny

3 MOSES

Moses

Moses a mighty prophet of God was spared from death at birth and his mother hid him as long as she could. She placed him in a basket in the river rather than let him die. The scripture doesn't say she prayed, but I'm sure she prayed over her child as she let the basket float on the river not knowing where it would go. The princess was bathing and heard the child crying and took him unto herself and raised him as her own child.

Exodus 2:1 Now a man of the tribe of Levi married a Levite woman, 2 and she became pregnant and gave birth to a son. When she saw that he was a fine child, she hid him for three months. 3 But when she could hide him no longer, she got a papyrus basket[a] for him and coated it with tar and pitch. Then she placed the child in it and put it among the reeds along the bank of the Nile. 4 His sister stood at a distance to see what would happen to him.

5 Then Pharaoh's daughter went down to the Nile to bathe, and her attendants were walking along the riverbank. She saw the basket among the reeds and sent her female slave to get it. 6 She opened it and

saw the baby. He was crying, and she felt sorry for him. "This is one of the Hebrew babies," she said.

7 Then his sister asked Pharaoh's daughter, "Shall I go and get one of the Hebrew women to nurse the baby for you?"

8 "Yes, go," she answered. So the girl went and got the baby's mother. 9 Pharaoh's daughter said to her, "Take this baby and nurse him for me, and I will pay you." So the woman took the baby and nursed him. 10 When the child grew older, she took him to Pharaoh's daughter and he became her son. She named him Moses,[b] saying, "I drew him out of the water."

God not only saved Moses' life but got his Hebrew mother to wean him. He was raised to a high position as a prince in Egypt getting the best education, training, skills and opportunities. God's blessing on him preserved his life and promoted him to a prestigious position. He rose to prominence – but became an outlaw because of his killing of an Egyptian who was beating an Israelite.

Exodus 2: 11 One day, after Moses had grown up, he went out to where his own people were and watched them at their hard labor. He saw an Egyptian beating a Hebrew, one of his own people. 12 Looking this way and that and seeing no one, he killed the Egyptian and hid him in the sand. ¹³ The next day he went out and saw two Hebrews fighting. He asked the one in the wrong, "Why are you hitting your fellow Hebrew?"

¹⁴ The man said, "Who made you ruler and judge over us? Are you thinking of killing me as you killed the Egyptian?" Then Moses was afraid and thought, "What I did must have become known."

¹⁵ When Pharaoh heard of this, he tried to kill Moses, but Moses fledf rom Pharaoh and went to live in Midian, where he sat down by a well. ¹⁶ Now a priest of Midian had seven daughters, and they came to draw water and fill the troughs to water their father's flock. ¹⁷ Some shepherds came along and drove them away, but Moses got up and came to their rescue and watered their flock.

²¹ Moses agreed to stay with the man, who gave his daughter Zipporahto Moses in marriage. ²² Zipporah gave birth to a son, and Moses named him Gershom,[c] saying, "I have become a foreigner in a foreign land."

Banished from Israel, Moses wandered through the Sinai desert until he got to the land of Midian. There he rested and made his living as a shepherd for forty years. He married, had children, lived and ordinary life. All the Hebrews were in Egypt, still in slavery, praying for deliverance.

Exodus 2: ²³ During that long period, the king of Egypt died. The Israelites groaned in their slavery and cried out, and their cry for help because of their slavery went up to God. ²⁴ God heard their groaning and he remembered his covenant with Abraham, with Isaac and with Jacob. ²⁵ So God looked on the Israelites and was concerned about them.

God reveals Himself to Moses

God revealed himself to Moses in a special way. Because he was a shepherd. God appeared as a bush that was burning but did not burn out. It is normal for sagebrush to instantly combust, but it always burns out quickly. The bush did not burn out. Moses got curious and climbed a mountain to try to understand the burning bush. There he encountered God's presence and was called to be a deliverer of Israel out of Egypt.

Exodus 3: ² There the angel of the LORD appeared to him in flames of fire from within a bush. Moses saw that though the bush was on fire it did not burn up. ³ So Moses thought, "I will go over and see this strange sight—why the bush does not burn up."

⁴ When the Lord saw that he had gone over to look, God called to him from within the bush, "Moses! Moses!"

And Moses said, "Here I am."

⁵ "Do not come any closer," God said. "Take off your sandals, for the place where you are standing is holy ground." ⁶ Then he said, "I am the God of your father,[a] the God of Abraham, the God of Isaac and the God of Jacob." At this, Moses hid his face, because he was afraid to look at God.

⁷ The Lord said, "I have indeed seen the misery of my people in Egypt. I have heard them crying out because of their slave drivers, and I am concerned about their suffering. ⁸ So I have come down to rescue them from the hand of the Egyptians and to bring them up out of that land into a good and spacious land, a land flowing with milk and honey—the home of the Canaanites, Hittites, Amorites, Perizzites, Hivites and Jebusites. ⁹ And now the cry of the Israelites has reached me, and I have seen the way the Egyptians are oppressing them. ¹⁰ So now, go. I am sending you to Pharaoh to bring my people the Israelites out of Egypt."

Moses first response was not faith. He listed all his weaknesses to God as to why he should not be considered as leader for such a huge task as delivering two million Israelites from Egyptian bondage. God commanded him to use the supernatural signs to show to Pharaoh so that Pharaoh would know God was speaking through Moses. God allowed Moses to bring his brother Aaron to assist him as Moses did not feel he could speak with eloquence. God could have used Moses and shone the glory of God through him without any other person, but God comforted Moses by letting him bring Aaron.

Moses and Aaron go to Egypt

Moses and Aaron went to Egypt and Moses appeared before Pharaoh and commanded that the Israelites be set free to worship their God. Miracles signs wonders occurred. There were 10 plagues upon Egypt because Pharaoh's heart was hard and did not want to let Israel go free. The plague would occur, Pharaoh would beg Moses to stop it. As soon as it stopped, Pharaoh's heart hardened, and he would not let Israel go free. Finally, the last plague – the death of the first-born impacted Pharaoh personally with his own son's death. He let Israel go free. This is a miracle. A mighty powerful kingdom such as Egypt with technology and authority released 2, 000,000 Israelite slaves because of the God of Israel.

Exodus 12: ³¹During the night Pharaoh summoned Moses and Aaron and said, "Up! Leave my people, you and the Israelites! Go, worship the LORD as you have requested. ³²Take your flocks and herds, as you have said, and go. And also bless me."

³³The Egyptians urged the people to hurry and leave the country. "For otherwise," they said, "we will all die!" ³⁴So the people took their dough before the yeast was added, and carried it on their shoulders in kneading troughs wrapped in clothing. ³⁵The Israelites did as Moses instructed and asked the Egyptians for articles of silver and gold and for clothing. ³⁶The LORD had made the Egyptians favorably disposed toward the people, and they gave them what they asked for; so they plundered the Egyptians.

There was not enough time to make a proper dinner. The Israelites got the word they were free, and they hurried packing their belongings, gathering their stuff and preparing to leave to go to the land that God promised Abraham. Israel over 2,000, 000 of them with flocks and herds and spoils of Egypt were set free. Moses lead them. God used Moses and Aaron. God spoke with Moses as friend with friend. God sovereignly provided water, food for the Israelites as they travelled through the desert.

The origin of modern Judaism

God gave the commandments to Moses at Mt Sinai and they were God's instructions for how the Israelites could live pleasing lives to God. They were commandments for living a life of blessing and God's favour. It was the start of Judaism. God gave Moses the Levitical laws (613 of them) that governed all aspects of their lives including food, health, lifestyle, marriage, business, trade, worship, sacrifice, festivals, religion beliefs, etc. Keeping them meant that God would bless the people with the blessing of Abraham, Isaac and Jacob.

God chose Israel to reveal the commandments to – God chose Israel to worship Him. There were many other nations. God promised Abraham, Isaac, Jacob and Joseph and was leading the Israelites through Moses and Aaron to the land of promise. They carried Joseph's remains as Joseph had requested at his death. Joseph knew Israel would go to Canaan again. A patch of earth – promised to Abraham was the destiny of Israel; it is the destiny of Israel, will always belong to Israel because of God's covenant with Israel.

Israel was out of Egypt, but the Israelites were not wholly following God. Even though they were witnesses to all the miracles including the parting of the Red Sea so they could walk on dry ground through the midst of it, the people grumbled, complained and falsely accused Moses of leading them to their deaths. Rather than request that God give them water to drink and bread and food, they complained against God and Moses. Many preachers refer to Israel that wandered in the wilderness as Egypt was still in the Israelites. They were carnal. They did not know God. God provided water from a rock. God gave them a rain of manna (meaning what is it) which was used to bake bread and other things much life flour. God sent a multitude of quail to them so they could get more than their fill. But God showed His anger at their unbelief. Should they have prayed with faith, God would have supplied for them. Because they were sinning in their unbelief and accusations against God's servant Moses, God punished them with judgements until Moses and Aaron would run through the crowd praying and interceding for the people's lives. The people did not know how to live for God because they had been slaves in Egypt for 400 years. They believed in God but did not know Him or how to live for Him.

Exodus 16: [11] The LORD said to Moses, [12] "I have heard the grumbling of the Israelites. Tell them, 'At twilight you will eat meat, and in the morning you will be filled with bread. Then you will know that I am the LORD your God.'"

[13] That evening quail came and covered the camp, and in the morning there was a layer of dew around the camp. [14] When the dew was gone, thin flakes like frost on the ground appeared on the desert floor. [15] When the Israelites saw it, they said to each other, "What is it?" For they did not know what it was.

Moses said to them, "It is the bread the LORD has given you to eat. [16] This is what the LORD has commanded: 'Everyone is to gather as much as they need. Take an omer[a] for each person you have in your tent.'"

[17] The Israelites did as they were told; some gathered much, some little. [18] And when they measured it by the omer, the one who gathered much did not have too much, and the one who gathered little did not have too little. Everyone had gathered just as much as they needed.

[19] Then Moses said to them, "No one is to keep any of it until morning."

    God brought water from the rock. Moses obeyed God and struck the rock and water gushed out. God supernaturally supplied for Israel all during the journey through the wilderness.

Exodus 17: ⁵The LORD answered Moses, "Go out in front of the people. Take with you some of the elders of Israel and take in your hand the staff with which you struck the Nile, and go. ⁶I will stand there before you by the rock at Horeb. Strike the rock, and water will come out of it for the people to drink." So Moses did this in the sight of the elders of Israel.⁷And he called the place Massah[a] and Meribah[b] because the Israelites quarreled and because they tested the LORD saying, "Is the LORD among us or not?"

The Commandments

God gave the commandments to Moses so the people would know how to live. They are known as the decalogue or essential rules for life. Christians and Jews both believe in them as the foundational rules of society. These and the other Levitical laws (613) established a way of living in all manner of human existence. God revealed His will to the people and gave instructions for life through the Torah. They are the basis for which all Israeli and Western culture established our laws and lifestyle. They are the foundation on which North America was built. They were once posted in schools and public places. They were memorized by school children as a way of living. God's Word is the moral code of Western Society. The commandments and laws free us to live pleasing to God. As we honour God by keeping them, He blesses us.

Sin is the transgression or not keeping of the commandments. There was necessity to establish an atonement for sin because people as much as they desire to please God cannot do it on their own. Animal sacrifice was established for Israel. The animal's life was offered as a sacrifice; it did not erase the sin but covered it. I compare it to white out covering over text errors. Underneath, it was there. God promised a Messiah would come who would cleanse all of Israel from all sin and would live with us and we would be His people ands He would be our God and we would no longer sin because our hearts would be changed by Him.
The commandments are the most essential aspects of human life. They cover man's relationship with God and man's relationships with each other.

> Exodus 20 [2] "I am the LORD your God, who brought you out of Egypt, out of the land of slavery.

[3] "You shall have no other gods before[a] me.

[4] "You shall not make for yourself an image in the form of anything in heaven above or on the earth beneath or in the waters below. [5] You shall not bow down to them or worship them; for I, the LORD your God, am a jealous

God, punishing the children for the sin of the parents to the third and fourth generation of those who hate me, ⁶but showing love to a thousand generations of those who love me and keep my commandments.

⁷"You shall not misuse the name of the Lord your God, for the Lord will not hold anyone guiltless who misuses his name.

⁸"Remember the Sabbath day by keeping it holy. ⁹Six days you shall labor and do all your work, ¹⁰but the seventh day is a sabbath to the Lord your God. On it you shall not do any work, neither you, nor your son or daughter, nor your male or female servant, nor your animals, nor any foreigner residing in your towns. ¹¹For in six days the Lord made the heavens and the earth, the sea, and all that is in them, but he rested on the seventh day. Therefore, the Lord blessed the Sabbath day and made it holy.

¹²"Honor your father and your mother, so that you may live long in the land the Lord your God is giving you.

¹³"You shall not murder.

¹⁴"You shall not commit adultery.

¹⁵"You shall not steal.

16 "You shall not give false testimony against your neighbor.

17 "You shall not covet your neighbor's house. You shall not covet your neighbor's wife, or his male or female servant, his ox or donkey, or anything that belongs to your neighbor."

Animal sacrifice was established for atonement from sin. With it there was worship and praise and thanksgiving for God 's provision for us so we could rejoice in the blessings of God. It was necessary that all the people learned the commandments and the Levitical laws. Only in knowing them and keeping them could they lives pleasing to God. The altar of sacrifice was simple earth– with no engraving or any type of man-made decoration on it.

Exodus 20: 24 "'Make an altar of earth for me and sacrifice on it your burnt offerings and fellowship offerings, your sheep and goats and your cattle. Wherever I cause my name to be honored, I will come to you and bless you.

Aaron and his family are anointed as priests

The tribe of Levi was chosen by God to be the priests. They would teach the people the laws and they would offer the sacrifices and carry the holy things and be a separate people, consecrated to God.

Leviticus 8:
⁵ Moses said to the assembly, "This is what the LORD has commanded to be done." ⁶ Then Moses brought Aaron and his sons forward and washed them with water. ⁷ He put the tunic on Aaron, tied the sash around him, clothed him with the robe and put the ephod on him. He also fastened the ephod with a decorative waistband, which he tied around him. ⁸ He placed the breast piece on him and put the Urim and Thummim in the breast piece. ⁹ Then he placed the turban on Aaron's head and set the gold plate, the sacred emblem, on the front of it, as the LORD commanded Moses.

¹⁰ Then Moses took the anointing oil and anointed the tabernacle and everything in it, and so consecrated them. ¹¹ He sprinkled some of the oil on the altar seven times, anointing the altar and all its utensils and the basin with its stand, to consecrate them. ¹² He poured some of the anointing oil on Aaron's head and anointed him to consecrate him. ¹³ Then he brought Aaron's sons forward, put tunics on them, tied sashes around them and fastened caps on them, as the LORD commanded Moses.

³⁰ Then Moses took some of the anointing oil and some of the blood from the altar and sprinkled them on Aaron and his

garments and on his sons and their garments. So he consecrated Aaron and his garments and his sons and their garments.

Judaism was established and Aaron and his family were consecrated as the priests. The tribe of Levi was consecrated to God meaning they did not own land of their own so they could wholly minister to God, so they lived by the offerings of the people.

The Ark of the covenant

God told Moses to construct the ark of the covenant. It was a place He would place His Holy Presence. Moses obeyed God and Aaron and the priests carried it from one place to the next. The people worshipped God. It was not a symbol of God – It was the very presence of God dwelling with Israel. God chose to dwell in their midst.

God made covenants with Israel. God keeps His covenant. There was condition to inheriting the promises.

Exodus 11: [8] Observe therefore all the commands I am giving you today, so that you may have the strength to go in and take over the land that you are crossing the Jordan to possess, [9] and so that you may live long in the land the LORD swore to your ancestors to give to them and their descendants, a land flowing with milk and honey. [10] The land you are entering to take over is not like the land of Egypt, from which you have come, where you planted your seed and irrigated it by foot as in a vegetable garden. [11] But the land you are crossing the Jordan to take possession of is a land of mountains and valleys that drinks rain from heaven. [12] It is a land the LORD your God cares for; the eyes of the LORD your God are continually on it from the beginning of the year to its end.

[13] So if you faithfully obey the commands I am giving you today—to love the LORD your God and to serve him with all your heart and with all your soul— [14] then I will send rain on your land in its season, both autumn and spring rains, so that you may gather in your grain, new wine and olive oil. [15] I will provide grass in the fields for your cattle, and you will eat and be satisfied.

[16] Be careful, or you will be enticed to turn away and worship other gods and bow down to them. [17] Then the LORD's anger will burn against you, and he will shut up the heavens so that it will not rain and the ground will yield no produce, and you will soon perish from the good land the LORD is giving you. [18] Fix these words of mine in your hearts and minds; tie them as symbols on your hands and bind them on your foreheads. [19] Teach them to your children, talking about them when you sit at home and when you walk along the road, when you lie

down and when you get up. [20] Write them on the doorframes of your houses and on your gates, [21] so that your days and the days of your children may be many in the land the LORD swore to give your ancestors, as many as the days that the heavens are above the earth.

[22] If you carefully observe all these commands I am giving you to follow—to love the LORD your God, to walk in obedience to him and to hold fast to him— [23] then the LORD will drive out all these nations before you, and you will dispossess nations larger and stronger than you. [24] Every place where you set your foot will be yours: Your territory will extend from the desert to Lebanon, and from the Euphrates River to the Mediterranean Sea. [25] No one will be able to stand against you. The LORD your God, as he promised you, will put the terror and fear of you on the whole land, wherever you go.

5 MOSAIC COVENANT

God's commandments to Israel meant a life of blessing but there were also warnings concerning not keeping of them. There were blessings but also curses. Within the protection and blessing of obeying God's commandments people would prosper. Stepping outside the protection of God, by willfully sinning, meant the curse of Adam – consequences of sin. The commandments were given to Israel but all who believe in Jesus Christ know and obey the commandments because Jesus did. Jesus honoured God in all his ways.

Exodus 11: [26] See, I am setting before you today a blessing and a curse— [27] the blessing if you obey the commands of the LORD your God that I am giving you today; [28] the curse if you disobey the commands of the LORD your God and turn from the way that I command you today by following other gods, which you have not known.

The blessings of obeying God's covenant covered all aspects of human life. It meant God's blessing on them in every place they went as well as on their families, their children, their crops, their animals, supernatural protection and provision. It was the blessing of Abraham continued and made specific. The blessing applies to Israel but it also applies to all believers in Jesus because through Jesus Christ all the blessings are ours by faith.

Blessings for Obedience

Deuteronomy 28 If you fully obey the Lord your God and carefully follow all his commands I give you today, the Lord your God will set you high above all the nations on earth. ² All these blessings will come on you and accompany you if you obey the Lord your God:

³ You will be blessed in the city and blessed in the country.

⁴ The fruit of your womb will be blessed, and the crops of your land and the young of your livestock—the calves of your herds and the lambs of your flocks.

⁵ Your basket and your kneading trough will be blessed.

⁶ You will be blessed when you come in and blessed when you go out.

⁷ The Lord will grant that the enemies who rise up against you will be defeated before you. They will come at you from one direction but flee from you in seven.

⁸The LORD will send a blessing on your barns and on everything you put your hand to. The LORD your God will bless you in the land he is giving you.

⁹The LORD will establish you as his holy people, as he promised you on oath, if you keep the commands of the LORD your God and walk in obedience to him. ¹⁰Then all the peoples on earth will see that you are called by the name of the LORD, and they will fear you. ¹¹The LORD will grant you abundant prosperity—in the fruit of your womb, the young of your livestock and the crops of your ground—in the land he swore to your ancestors to give you.

¹²The LORD will open the heavens, the storehouse of his bounty, to send rain on your land in season and to bless all the work of your hands. You will lend to many nations but will borrow from none. ¹³The LORD will make you the head, not the tail. If you pay attention to the commands of the LORD your God that I give you this day and carefully follow them, you will always be at the top, never at the bottom. ¹⁴Do not turn aside from any of the commands I give you today, to the right or to the left, following other gods and serving them.

      Disobedience to God means living with the curse of the law. It meant the opposite of the blessing. Those who sinned against God stepped from out of the blessing and protection of God. It means they no longer have the blessing of God on their lives. That is why we must repent quickly if we sin. Repentance brings forgiveness and restoration. We can once more enjoy the blessings of God by obeying Him and keeping our hearts pure.

Exodus 28: ¹⁵ However, if you do not obey the LORD your God and do not carefully follow all his commands and decrees I am giving you today, all these curses will come on you and overtake you:

The list of curses is long (Deut. 28). The curse is not new. It is the same curse that was on Adam for sinning. Living outside of the realm of God's protection means living without the blessing. It means toil, thorns, thistles, separation from God.

Promises made to Abraham and Moses – apply today to modern Israel. They belong to all who believe in Christ because by faith in Jesus we have peace with God and are children of the covenant.

Deuteronomy 7: ⁹ Know therefore that the LORD your God is God; he is the faithful God, keeping his covenant of love to a thousand generations of those who love him and keep his commandments. ¹⁰ But those who hate him he will repay to their face by destruction;

he will not be slow to repay to their face those who hate him.

¹¹Therefore, take care to follow the commands, decrees and laws I give you today.

God would bless the people or the people would chose to sin and receive the curse of sin – separation from God and the loss of the blessing. This is true of Israel. It is also true of all Christians because through Jesus Christ the blessings of Abraham come.

Exodus 20: 6 **for I, the LORD your God, am a jealous God, punishing the children for the sin of the parents to the third and fourth generation of those who hate me,** ⁶**but showing love to a thousand generations of those who love me and keep my commandments.**

At the edge of the promised land

After a week or so of their desert life, they approached the promised land. Moses chose 12 spies who would go into the promised land and bring back a report to him.

Ten spies brought back an evil report. That means they reported that yes the promised land was lush, bountiful, with produce and steams etc. but the people were giants and they feared the people – they were not trusting in God to give them victory. Their report was of no faith in God. Joshua and Caleb were the only ones who brought a good report. They talked of the huge fruits and vegetables – described it as a land of milk and honey and both proclaimed that they should enter in immediately because they believed God would give them the victory. The Israelites refused to go into the promised land; it was unbelief - sin. They did not believe the God who had delivered them from Egypt would give them the promised land. This resulting in God's judgement of them and because of it none of those people who believed the negative report lived to enter the promised land. For forty years they wandered in the wilderness. God provided for them, but they could not receive from God the promised land because they did not believe. They died in the wilderness not possessing what God had promised them.

Faith

Joshua and Caleb were the only spies who lived to enter the promised land because they believed God was able to give them the land. Moses drew near to the promised land but did not enter. He had sinned by displaying anger at the Israelites unbelief and through his anger, he disobeyed God. God instructed Him to sing to the rock to receive water but he in his anger struck the rock (as he had done on other occasions). It is a severe judgement on Moses who in all other ways did not disobey God, but a leader must live beyond all reproach and he was the leader of millions of people. Obedience to God is more important than anything else. God does not always instruct someone the same way. God is not religious. He is Spirit.

John 4: 24 God is spirit, and his worshipers must worship in the Spirit and in truth."

Moses led the people forty years through the wilderness to the edge of the promised land and anointed Joshua to lead them into the promised land. God chose Joshua who obeyed God and served Moses for many years. He was one of the spies who believed God could deliver the land to Israel. Moses imparted a blessing to Joshua. He prayed over him.

Exodus 7: 7 Then Moses summoned Joshua and said to him in the presence of all Israel, "Be strong and courageous, for you must go with this people into the land that the LORD swore to their ancestors to give them, and you must divide it among them as their inheritance. 8 The LORD himself goes before you and will be with you; he will never leave you nor forsake you. Do not be afraid; do not be discouraged."

The blessing imparted

At the entry to the promised land Moses prayed over Joshua and imparted to him the blessing and he prayed Joshua would successfully lead the people into the promised land. This type of prayer is known as the mantle passed on, that is the blessing or anointing on one leader is imparted – spiritually – as well as publicly to the next leader. Moses warned Joshua that Israel would not always serve God. He commanded them to keep God's commandments. God gave Moses a long song about the deliverance of Israel out of Egypt and their heritage. It was a way all the people of Israel could pass on to their children the truths of God.

Joshua

Joshua lead Israel into battles to possess the promised land. It was the land that Abraham was promised and eventually possessed. It was their heritage and their destiny. God was the strategist of all the battles. God gave instructions to Joshua on how to lead the battle. The instructions may seem peculiar, but they always resulted in victory for the Israelites. The main ingredient was faith. Israel obeyed God and the results were victory. Israel did not obey God and there was loss. For example, in taking the city of Jericho, God instructed them to march around the city.

Joshua 6: ³March around the city once with all the armed men. Do this for six days. ⁴Have seven priests carry trumpets of rams' horns in front of the ark. On the seventh day, march around the city seven times, with the priests blowing the trumpets. ⁵When you hear them sound a long blast on the trumpets, have the whole army give a loud shout; then the wall of the city will collapse and the army will go up, everyone straight in."

The Israelites obeyed and because of it, the walls of Jericho came tumbling down. The Israelites had a strong victory there. Thirty-one kings were conquered, and the Israelites possessed the promised land. The instructions for each battle were different. Joshua obeyed God and lead the people. He kept all that Moses had taught them and honoured God in all his ways. Because of it, the people honoured God and served Him. One of the most awesome parts of Joshua is that he designated the land to the twelve tribes.

Joshua warned Israel not to depart from God or God would judge them for it. All of Joshua's life Israel served God and prospered.

Joshua 24: ³¹Israel served the LORD throughout the lifetime of Joshua and of the elders who outlived him and who had experienced everything the Lord had done for Israel.

After Joshua

After the death of Joshua, there were leaders who served God; there were also rulers who did not. Because of some of the rulers were not serving God, there were wars and fighting and judgements on Israel. Some of the leaders set up idol worship – totally against God's commandments.

6 KINGS OF ISRAEL

Kings of Israel

There were prophets of God who rose to prominence; they spoke God's Word and condemned sin. The people of Israel wanted a king like the other nations around them. The prophet Samuel was God's chosen leader of Israel. He obeyed God and spoke to the people. God gave the people a king as they desired. The next leader to arise in Israel that God made special covenant with was King David. The first King, Saul had sinned against God and did not repent so God took his blessing off his life. King David was a shepherd and the youngest of his family. The prophet Samuel anointed him as king before he was the king. It was many years before he would become the king but not long until he started being prepared for life in the palace.

1 Samuel 16: Then the LORD said, "Rise and anoint him; this is the one."

[13] So Samuel took the horn of oil and anointed him in the presence of his brothers, and from that day on the Spirit of the LORD came powerfully upon David. Samuel then went to Ramah.

King Saul was plagued by evil spirits and David played the harp and sang. It caused there to be peace for Saul. David also was strong in his believing in God. He took on the giant Goliath and defeated him. 1 Samuel 42- 51. He was raised up and promoted to a high rank in the army of Israel.

1 Samuel 18: **⁵Whatever mission Saul sent him on, David was so successful that Saul gave him a high rank in the army. This pleased all the troops, and Saul's officers as well.**

David was wise and humble. He served God first and served Saul with all his being loyally, but Saul grew jealous of David's reputation. David excelled at all areas in which he was given responsibility. This was the blessing of God on his life. Saul grew so jealous (of the blessing of God) he tried to kill David with a spear. David had married Saul's daughter and become best friends with Johnathon his son. He was as part of the family, but Saul's evil spirits hated the blessing on David's life. Saul began to chase David to kill him accusing him of being disloyal. It was a lie. David was innocent yet he spent years fleeing from Saul's attacks on his life. He was hunted as though he were a criminal, but David did not try to attack Saul though he had the chance, more than once, to kill him.

David pretended to be loyal to an enemy army, but he would attack the enemy towns and villages and leave none of them living. He was loyal both to Saul and Israel at the risk of his own life because Saul was trying to kill him. Saul became so possessed by the evil spirits, he could not hear from God. He went to a witch to get her to conjure up the spirit of the Prophet Samuel because he wanted guidance for his army and the wars that he was facing. In that battle the next day he was killed. God's presence was no longer with Saul and Saul did not know what to do. That day Saul was told he would lose his life the next day in battle. There was a terrible loss for Israel and a victory of the Philistines.

1 Samuel 31: [7] When the Israelites along the valley and those across the Jordan saw that the Israelite army had fled and that Saul and his sons had died, they abandoned their towns and fled. And the Philistines came and occupied them.

[8] The next day, when the Philistines came to strip the dead, they found Saul and his three sons fallen on Mount Gilboa. [9] They cut off his head and stripped off his armor, and they sent messengers throughout the land of the Philistines to proclaim the news in the temple of their idols and among their people. [10] They put his armor in the temple of the Ashtoreth's and fastened his body to the wall of Beth Shan.

Israel our Christian Heritage: Israel our Christian Destiny

7 DAVID BECOMES KING

David did not presume to take the leadership of Israel. Even though he had been anointed king, he prayed asking God to lead him. God was with him and directed him. David had relationship with God.

2 Samuel 2:1 In the course of time, David inquired of the LORD. "Shall I go up to one of the towns of Judah?" he asked.

The LORD said, "Go up."

David asked, "Where shall I go?"

"To Hebron," the LORD answered.

² So David went up there with his two wives, Ahinoam of Jezreel and Abigail, the widow of Nabal of Carmel. ³ David also took the men who were with him, each with his family, and they settled in Hebron and its towns. ⁴ Then the men of Judah came to Hebron, and there they anointed David king over the tribe of Judah.

David honoured God and because of it, not long after becoming king of Judah, David became king over all of Israel. He worshipped God and wrote many of the Psalms as songs of worship to God.

2 Samuel 5:1 All the tribes of Israel came to David at Hebron and said, "We are your own flesh and blood. ² In the past, while Saul was king over us, you were the one who led Israel on their military campaigns. And the LORD said to you, 'You will shepherd my people Israel, and you will become their ruler.'"

³ When all the elders of Israel had come to King David at Hebron, the king made a covenant with them at Hebron before the LORD, and they anointed David king over Israel.

⁴ David was thirty years old when he became king, and he reigned forty years. ⁵ In Hebron he reigned over Judah seven years and six months, and in Jerusalem he reigned over all Israel and Judah thirty-three years.

Israel prospered with David as their king because his heart was serving God.

He worshipped God openly and brought the ark of the covenant to Jerusalem. He re-established Levitical sacrifice and praise and worship. The people followed God because of him.

He desired to build a temple for God, but God did not let him. God instructed him that his son would build the temple. David collected all the materials and set aside money to build the temple. He imparted into his son a desire for God and a desire to complete the temple. God did not let him build a temple but promised him his son would. God promised David that as long as his descendants would serve God, He would prosper them and there would always be kings established through his lineage. It is through his lineage Jesus Christ came.

2 Samuel 7: ¹²When your days are over and you rest with your ancestors, I will raise up your offspring to succeed you, your own flesh and blood, and I will establish his kingdom. ¹³He is the one who will build a house for my Name, and I will establish the throne of his kingdom forever.

Solomon built the temple

The building of the temple is highly significant in more than one way. It was a permanent dwelling place for the ark of the covenant. It was God's promise that Israel would be God's people and He would dwell with them and they would be his people and He would be their God. God chose to dwell, His Spirit present with them, in Jerusalem with Israel. It was a gathering place for all of Israel so they could worship together and celebrate feasts together. It brought strength to Israel and peace because all of Israel served God while the Kings were serving God. It was the fulfillment of the promises made to Abraham, God's living presence with the people. Solomon wholly followed God in building the temple. He got all the stuff and hired the most skillful people. It took 7 years to accomplish. Those were his best years as king.

1 Kings 6:1 In the four hundred and eightieth[a] year after the Israelites came out of Egypt, in the fourth year of Solomon's reign over Israel, in the month of Ziv, the second month, he began to build the temple of the LORD.

The temple was built, and special care was given to each part of it as God instructed. It was beautiful, magnificent and excellent. The best materials had been gathered. The craftsmen were experts gifted in all kinds of specialty carving and creating. It was giving God the best of all things to magnify Him.

1 Kings 6: [19] He prepared the inner sanctuary within the temple to set the ark of the covenant of the LORD there. [20] The inner sanctuary was twenty cubits long, twenty wide and twenty high. He overlaid the inside with pure gold, and he also overlaid the altar of cedar. [21] Solomon covered the inside of the temple with pure gold, and he extended gold chains across the front of the inner sanctuary, which was overlaid with gold. [22] So he overlaid the

whole interior with gold. He also overlaid with gold the altar that belonged to the inner sanctuary.

[23] For the inner sanctuary he made a pair of cherubim out of olive wood, each ten cubits high. [24] One wing of the first cherub was five cubits long, and the other wing five cubits—ten cubits from wing tip to wing tip. [25] The second cherub also measured ten cubits, for the two cherubim were identical in size and shape. [26] The height of each cherub was ten cubits. [27] He placed the cherubim inside the innermost room of the temple, with their wings spread out. The wing of one cherub touched one wall, while the wing of the other touched the other wall, and their wings touched each other in the middle of the room. [28] He overlaid the cherubim with gold.

It is meaningful. The ark of the covenant, the dwelling place of God, was placed within the temple. The God of Israel who promised to dwell with His people, had a special place. It was the temple at Jerusalem. The people knew the blessing was passed on; they knew Moses leadership and were taught by the Levites. The temple was nothing but a beautiful building until the presence of God was brought in - in the ark of the covenant.

1 Kings 8: [3] When all the elders of Israel had arrived, the priests took up the ark, [4] and they brought up the

ark of the LORD and the tent of meeting and all the sacred furnishings in it. The priests and Levites carried them up,⁵ and King Solomon and the entire assembly of Israel that had gathered about him were before the ark, sacrificing so many sheep and cattle that they could not be recorded or counted.

⁶ The priests then brought the ark of the LORD's covenant to its place in the inner sanctuary of the temple, the Most Holy Place, and put it beneath the wings of the cherubim. ⁷ The cherubim spread their wings over the place of the ark and overshadowed the ark and its carrying poles. ⁸ These poles were so long that their ends could be seen from the Holy Place in front of the inner sanctuary, but not from outside the Holy Place; and they are still there today. ⁹ There was nothing in the ark except the two stone tablets that Moses had placed in it at Horeb, where the LORD made a covenant with the Israelites after they came out of Egypt.

¹⁰ When the priests withdrew from the Holy Place, the cloud filled the temple of the LORD. ¹¹ And the priests could not perform their service because of the cloud, for the glory of the LORD filled his temple.

God's presence brought the glory of God in the temple and people could see the visible glory of God on the structure. Although it was beautiful as a structure – the best that man could give to God, it became overwhelmingly beautiful with the glory of God's presence in it.

1 Kings 8: ⁶²Then the king and all Israel with him offered sacrifices before the LORD. ⁶³Solomon offered a sacrifice of fellowship offerings to the LORD: twenty-two thousand cattle and a hundred and twenty thousand sheep and goats. So the king and all the Israelites dedicated the temple of the LORD.

Judaism had full expression. They worshipped God in Jerusalem. The presence of God was there. The people knew God was with them because His Holy presence was there. The Word of God was taught and preached by the Levites. The sacrifices were offered. People worshipped God. They honoured God.

Solomon's prayer over the Temple at dedication

Solomon's prayer of dedication covers all aspects of human life. Any sin that might be committed, could be forgiven. His prayer was that any who truly repented could always be forgiven. This is the essence of God's promises to Moses. Should Israel keep the commandments, Israel would always be blessed. Should Israel sin and repent, God would forgive her.

1 Kings 8: [22] Then Solomon stood before the altar of the LORD in front of the whole assembly of Israel, spread out his hands toward heaven [23] and said:

"LORD, the God of Israel, there is no God like you in heaven above or on earth below—you who keep your covenant of love with your servants who continue wholeheartedly in your way. [24] You have kept your promise to your servant David my father; with your mouth you have promised and with your hand you have fulfilled it—as it is today.

[25] "Now LORD, the God of Israel, keep for your servant David my father the promises you made to him when you said, 'You shall never fail to have a successor to sit before me on the throne of Israel, if only your descendants are careful in all they do to walk before me faithfully as you have done.' [26] And now, God of Israel, let your word that you promised your servant David my father come true.

[27] "But will God really dwell on earth? The heavens, even the highest heaven, cannot contain you. How much less this temple I have built! [28] Yet give attention to your servant's prayer and his plea for mercy, LORD my God. Hear the cry and the prayer that your servant is praying in your presence this day. [29] May your eyes be open toward this temple night and day, this place of which you said, 'My Name shall be there,' so that you will hear the prayer your servant prays toward this place. [30] Hear the

supplication of your servant and of your people Israel when they pray toward this place. Hear from heaven, your dwelling place, and when you hear, forgive.

31 "When anyone wrongs their neighbor and is required to take an oath and they come and swear the oath before your altar in this temple, 32 then hear from heaven and act. Judge between your servants, condemning the guilty by bringing down on their heads what they have done, and vindicating the innocent by treating them in accordance with their innocence.

33 "When your people Israel have been defeated by an enemy because they have sinned against you, and when they turn back to you and give praise to your name, praying and making supplication to you in this temple, 34 then hear from heaven and forgive the sin of your people Israel and bring them back to the land you gave to their ancestors.

35 "When the heavens are shut up and there is no rain because your people have sinned against you, and when they pray toward this place and give praise to your name and turn from their sin because you have afflicted them, 36 then hear from heaven and forgive the sin of your servants, your people Israel. Teach them the right way to live, and send rain on the land you gave your people for an inheritance.

37 "When famine or plague comes to the land, or blight or mildew, locusts or grasshoppers, or when an enemy besieges them in any of their cities, whatever disaster or disease may come, 38 and when a prayer or plea is made by anyone among your people Israel—being aware of the afflictions of their own hearts, and spreading out their hands toward this temple— 39 then hear from heaven, your dwelling place. Forgive and act; deal with everyone according to all they do, since you know their hearts (for you alone know every human heart), 40 so that they will fear you all the time they live in the land you gave our ancestors.

41 "As for the foreigner who does not belong to your people Israel but has come from a distant land because of your name— 42 for they will hear of your great name and your mighty hand and your outstretched arm—when they come and pray toward this temple, 43 then hear from heaven, your dwelling place. Do whatever the foreigner asks of you, so that all the peoples of the earth may know your name and fear you, as do your own people Israel, and may know that this house I have built bears your Name.

44 "When your people go to war against their enemies, wherever you send them, and when they pray to the LORD toward the city you have chosen and the temple I have built for your Name, 45 then hear from heaven their prayer and their plea, and uphold their cause.

⁴⁶ "When they sin against you—for there is no one who does not sin—and you become angry with them and give them over to their enemies, who take them captive to their own lands, far away or near; ⁴⁷ and if they have a change of heart in the land where they are held captive, and repent and plead with you in the land of their captors and say, 'We have sinned, we have done wrong, we have acted wickedly'; ⁴⁸ and if they turn back to you with all their heart and soul in the land of their enemies who took them captive, and pray to you toward the land you gave their ancestors, toward the city you have chosen and the temple I have built for your Name; ⁴⁹ then from heaven, your dwelling place, hear their prayer and their plea, and uphold their cause. ⁵⁰ And forgive your people, who have sinned against you; forgive all the offenses they have committed against you, and cause their captors to show them mercy; ⁵¹ for they are your people and your inheritance, whom you brought out of Egypt, out of that iron-smelting furnace.

⁵² "May your eyes be open to your servant's plea and to the plea of your people Israel, and may you listen to them whenever they cry out to you. ⁵³ For you singled them out from all the nations of the world to be your own inheritance, just as you declared through your servant Moses when you,
Sovereign LORD, brought our ancestors out of Egypt."

⁵⁴ When Solomon had finished all these prayers and supplications to the Lord, he rose from before the altar of the Lord, where he had been kneeling with his hands spread out toward heaven. ⁵⁵ He stood and blessed the whole assembly of Israel in a loud voice, saying:

⁵⁶ "Praise be to the Lord, who has given rest to his people Israel just as he promised. Not one word has failed of all the good promises he gave through his servant Moses. ⁵⁷ May the Lord our God be with us as he was with our ancestors; may he never leave us nor forsake us. ⁵⁸ May he turn our hearts to him, to walk in obedience to him and keep the commands, decrees and laws he gave our ancestors. ⁵⁹ And may these words of mine, which I have prayed before the Lord, be near to the Lord our God day and night, that he may uphold the cause of his servant and the cause of his people Israel according to each day's need, ⁶⁰ so that all the peoples of the earth may know that the Lord is God and that there is no other. ⁶¹ And may your hearts be fully committed to the Lord our God, to live by his decrees and obey his commands, as at this time."

Solomon's prayer covers the covenants of Israel. Solomon's heart is towards the people in his prayer he intercedes for them praying that God will always forgive them and bless them. The king interceding for the people is the ultimate type of earthly leadership. A king who honours God and prays for the people is a true leader. God protects them and honours their prayers.

2 Chronicles 7:1 When Solomon finished praying, fire came down from heaven and consumed the burnt offering and the sacrifices, and the glory of the LORD filled the temple. ²The priests could not enter the temple of the LORD because the glory of the LORD filled it. ³When all the Israelites saw the fire coming down and the glory of the LORD above the temple, they knelt on the pavement with their faces to the ground, and they worshiped and gave thanks to the LORD, saying,

"He is good;
  his love endures forever."

God's response to Solomon shows his approval of the Temple and of the dedication. God showed His mercy towards Israel by His dwelling in their midst. God's Holy presence was in the Ark of the Covenant in the Temple. People saw the glory of God fill the Temple. Israel knew that their God was real and that they were worshipping the true God. His presence is what made the difference.

1 Kings 9: ³The LORD said to him:

"I have heard the prayer and plea you have made before me; I have consecrated this temple, which you have built, by putting my Name there forever. My eyes and my heart will always be there.

    For many years, Israel knew God's blessing because of King David and Solomon. Once Solomon's mother died, he no longer served God but turned to idol worship because of his wives. God had promised to bless David's offspring and he did but they did not all serve God.

    Some of the kings served God. Some of the kings did not. Some kings worshipped God. Some lead Israel into idolatry. Prophets were people that God spoke with and instructed to speak to Israel. Prophets would warn the evil kings and direct the righteous kings. Prophets prophesied judgement and the destruction of the temple because of idolatry and sin. People's hearts were not circumcised. That means that although they partly obeyed God, they kept sinning because there was a hardness in their hearts because their sin nature was strong. They were carnal. They would sin, repent, sin repent etc. God's plan is that they would have the word of God written on their hearts and in their lives. Israel flourished and knew peace as the kings served God. As the kings no longer served God, there were wars and Israel suffered because of them.

Ezekiel 11: [19] I will give them an undivided heart and put a new spirit in them; I will remove from them their heart of stone and give them a heart of flesh. [20] Then they will follow my decrees and be careful to keep my laws. They will be my people, and I will be their God. [21] But as for those whose hearts are devoted to their vile images and detestable idols, I will bring down on their own heads what they have done, declares the Sovereign LORD."

Jeremiah 31: [33] "This is the covenant I will make with the people of Israel
   after that time," declares the LORD.
"I will put my law in their minds
   and write it on their hearts.
I will be their God,
   and they will be my people.

A Dual Nature

Animal sacrifice could not erase sin nature. It was the inherited sin of Adam and Eve. It was a divided self. The people wanted to serve God, but they enjoyed sinning. The two cannot remain together. God desires our hearts to be completely circumcised. God wants to be Lord of all our lives. Through faith in Jesus Christ, God's Holy Spirit wholly consumes the person. There is no longer a sin nature but a new nature – it is the life of Christ living in us in the presence of His Holy Spirit. Faith in Jesus Christ's shed blood means believing that Jesus died for our sins and He rose triumphantly over death, hell and the grave to give us victory in all areas of our lives. Jesus is the Messiah, the promised Saviour who cleanses us from all sin and erases it as though it never was there.

Hebrews 9: 11 But when Christ came as high priest of the good things that are now already here,[a] he went through the greater and more perfect tabernacle that is not made with human hands, that is to say, is not a part of this creation. 12 He did not enter by means of the blood of goats and calves; but he entered the Most Holy Place once for all by his own blood, thus obtaining[b] eternal redemption. ¹³ The blood of goats and bulls and the ashes of a heifer sprinkled on those who are ceremonially unclean sanctify them so that they are outwardly clean. ¹⁴ How much more, then, will the blood of Christ, who through the eternal Spirit offered himself unblemished to God, cleanse our consciences from acts that lead to death,[c] so that we may serve the living God!

Israel prophesied the coming of the Messiah would deliver Israel out of sin and would be a ruler. God's dwelling with Israel was a special part of the covenant He made with Israel. His Holy presence would be in their midst. They would keep his commandments and He would bless them. The book of Isaiah especially is dedicated to the coming Messiah that would atone for all sins but these prophecies concerning Jesus are throughout the Old Covenant.

8 THE DESTRUCTION OF THE TEMPLE

There were many kings after Solomon. In the later years of Solomon's life, he built temples to idols for his wives. It is a horrible truth. From his descendants many did not follow the Lord. There were some kings who served God and some who didn't. When the kings did not serve God, the people were swayed. Israel had become divided because of it. Judah remained loyal to King David's promise even though the kings were not all worshipping God. The rest of Israel served God, but they also had some good kings and bad kings. The results of the sins of Israel meant the curse. It meant living without protection or blessing from God. It led to the destruction of the temple as well as Jerusalem.

Jeremiah 39:1 **1 In the ninth year of Zedekiah king of Judah, in the tenth month, Nebuchadnezzar king of Babylon marched against Jerusalem with his whole army and laid siege to it. 2 And on the ninth day of the fourth month of Zedekiah's eleventh year, the city wall was broken through.**

8 The Babylonians[c] set fire to the royal palace and the houses of the people and broke down the walls of Jerusalem.

2 Kings 24: In the eighth year of the reign of the king of Babylon, he took Jehoiachin prisoner. ¹³As the L͟o͟r͟d͟ had declared, Nebuchadnezzar removed the treasures from the temple of the L͟o͟r͟d͟ and from the royal palace, and cut up the gold articles that Solomon king of Israel had made for the temple of the L͟o͟r͟d͟. ¹⁴He carried all Jerusalem into exile: all the officers and fighting men, and all the skilled workers and artisans—a total of ten thousand. Only the poorest people of the land were left.

9 DANIEL

Daniel was an Israelite taken to Babylon because he was young, handsome, strong, clever, intelligent. The Israeli youth who were wise and desirable were brought to Babylon and lived in the palace. Many other Israelites died or were taken as slaves. Daniel and his friends' lives in the palace was pleasant compared to the lives of many of the other Israelites after Babylon invaded Israel.

Daniel 1: [3] Then the king ordered Ashpenaz, chief of his court officials, to bring into the king's service some of the Israelites from the royal family and the nobility— [4] young men without any physical defect, handsome, showing aptitude for every kind of learning, well informed, quick to understand, and qualified to serve in the king's palace. He was to teach them the language and literature of the Babylonians.[b] [5] The king assigned them a daily amount of food and wine from the king's table. They were to be trained for three years, and after that they were to enter the king's service.
[6] Among those who were chosen were some from Judah: Daniel, Hananiah, Mishael and Azariah. [7] The chief official gave them new

names: to Daniel, the name Belteshazzar; to Hananiah, Shadrach; to Mishael, Meshach; and to Azariah, Abednego.

⁸But Daniel resolved not to defile himself with the royal food and wine, and he asked the chief official for permission not to defile himself this way.

¹⁷To these four young men God gave knowledge and understanding of all kinds of literature and learning. And Daniel could understand visions and dreams of all kinds.

      Hananiah, Azaria, Mesial, were special friends all of them servants of God. They would not eat the king's food because it was against the Levitical laws.
The scriptures do not allow the eating or drinking of blood. Their meat was bloody. They would not drink the wine because it was consecrated to the Babylonian pagan gods. God's blessing was on the Israelites because of their honouring of God.

Daniel interpreted dreams because it was a spiritual gift. He was prophetic in other ways also such as giving wise words and in intercessory prayer. Daniel and his friends were among the advisors to the king. Even though they were not free, the Israelites had impact on other nations by their honouring of God. God prospered them.

They would not bow to the golden idol Nebuchadnezzar built. Nebuchadnezzar built a huge statue to honour himself and made a law that people would bow to it in worship. He was proclaiming himself god. The Israelites would only worship the God of Israel. Nebuchadnezzar had them thrown into a fiery furnace to certain death because they would not bow to his idol.

Daniel 3: 8 At this time some astrologers[b] came forward and denounced the Jews. 9 They said to King Nebuchadnezzar, "May the king live forever! 10 Your Majesty has issued a decree that everyone who hears the sound of the horn, flute, zither, lyre, harp, pipe and all kinds of music must fall down and worship the image of gold, 11 and that whoever does not fall down and worship will be thrown into a blazing furnace. 12 But there are some Jews whom you have set over the affairs of the province of Babylon—Shadrach, Meshach and Abednego—who pay no attention to you, Your Majesty. They neither serve your gods nor worship the image of gold you have set up."

13 Furious with rage, Nebuchadnezzar summoned Shadrach, Meshach and Abednego. So these men were brought before the king, 14 and Nebuchadnezzar said to them, "Is it true, Shadrach, Meshach and Abednego, that you do not serve my gods or worship the image of gold I have set up? 15 Now when you hear the sound of the horn, flute, zither, lyre, harp,

pipe and all kinds of music, if you are ready to fall down and worship the image I made, very good. But if you do not worship it, you will be thrown immediately into a blazing furnace. Then what god will be able to rescue you from my hand?"

[16] Shadrach, Meshach and Abednego replied to him, "King Nebuchadnezzar, we do not need to defend ourselves before you in this matter. [17] If we are thrown into the blazing furnace, the God we serve is able to deliver us from it, and he will deliver us[c] from Your Majesty's hand. [18] But even if he does not, we want you to know, Your Majesty, that we will not serve your gods or worship the image of gold you have set up."

[24] Then King Nebuchadnezzar leaped to his feet in amazement and asked his advisers, "Weren't there three men that we tied up and threw into the fire?"

They replied, "Certainly, Your Majesty."

[25] He said, "Look! I see four men walking around in the fire, unbound and unharmed, and the fourth looks like a son of the gods."

[26] Nebuchadnezzar then approached the opening of the blazing furnace and shouted, "Shadrach, Meshach and Abednego, servants of the Most High God, come out! Come here!"

They were thrown in a furnace, but God preserved them. One like an angel appeared with them (many believe it was Jesus himself). They were walking around inside the fiery furnace. They were protected. There was no burning. They were as if they had not been thrown in. The king begged them to step out of the furnace and proclaimed their God as true God. They were appointed to high positions in the king's place.

Daniel and the lion's den

The new king's (Darius) magicians and soothsayers hated the Israelites because they were following the true God of Israel. They got the king to sign a declaration that no one could pray to anyone but the king. Daniel prayed to the God of Israel– and was arrested and sentenced to die in the Lion's den God sent an angel to preserve his life. The king sentenced their accusers to be thrown in the lion's den.

Daniel 6: [10] Now when Daniel learned that the decree had been published, he went home to his upstairs room where the windows opened toward Jerusalem. Three times a day he got down on his knees and prayed, giving thanks to his God, just as he had done before.

[16] So the king gave the order, and they brought Daniel and threw him into the lions'

den. The king said to Daniel, "May your God, whom you serve continually, rescue you!"

[21] Daniel answered, "May the king live forever! [22] My God sent his angel, and he shut the mouths of the lions. They have not hurt me, because I was found innocent in his sight. Nor have I ever done any wrong before you, Your Majesty."

[23] The king was overjoyed and gave orders to lift Daniel out of the den. And when Daniel was lifted from the den, no wound was found on him, because he had trusted in his God.

[24] At the king's command, the men who had falsely accused Daniel were brought in and thrown into the lions' den, along with their wives and children. And before they reached the floor of the den, the lions overpowered them and crushed all their bones.

Daniel was given special privilege and served three kings of Babylon as an adviser. God gave him special prophetic dreams regarding the end of the world as we know it – Daniel 7, 8, 9. These dreams affected him so much, he immediately began praying for the interpretation. Daniel prayed for 21 days regarding the meaning of the dreams. Finally, an angel came and spoke with him giving him the interpretation. They were prophetic dreams about the future and the kingdoms that would follow and their rulers.

Daniel's life is parallel to Joseph's because he was in a different country – a Gentile nation that didn't worship the true God, but he impacted the nation by the Spiritual anointing of God on his life. Because of him and his friends, Babylon had Godly wise council – Nebuchadnezzar came to know the true God of Israel.

Daniel 4: [34] At the end of that time, I, Nebuchadnezzar, raised my eyes toward heaven, and my sanity was restored. Then I praised the Most High; I honored and glorified him who lives forever.

His dominion is an eternal dominion;
   his kingdom endures from generation to generation.
[35] All the peoples of the earth
   are regarded as nothing.
He does as he pleases
   with the powers of heaven
   and the peoples of the earth.
No one can hold back his hand
   or say to him: "What have you done?"
[36] At the same time that my sanity was restored, my honor and splendor were returned to me for the glory of my kingdom. My advisers and nobles sought me out, and I was restored to my throne and became even greater than before. [37] Now I, Nebuchadnezzar, praise and exalt and glorify the King of heaven, because everything he does is right

and all his ways are just. And those who walk in pride he is able to humble.

Daniel's prophetic words validate prophecies in the book of Revelation and in other scriptures – concerning the end of the world. They were the prophetic dreams he was given with their interpretations.

God preserves a remnant – there is a remnant of believers even though the kings of Israel did not serve God, there were Israelites who did. It also shows God's concern for other nations in that God would use Israelites to give wisdom to those rulers and ultimately protect and keep his servants also.

God used the Gentiles to help rebuild Israel and the temple at Jerusalem. It was many years later but occurred. There is no direct word linking the events with the impact of the believing Jews in their midst, but I am sure the Israelites who honoured God impacted all of those around them. Those privileged to live in the king's palace had opportunity to impact rulers of nations.

10 THE REBUILDING OF THE TEMPLE NEHEMIAH, EZRA AND HAGGAI

Nehemiah was a servant of God, prophet of God, who worshipped God even though he was a wine taster for the king in Susa. They did not know God nor did they worship Him. But Nehemiah had such a blessing of God upon his life that he had the blessing of the King. Nehemiah knew that the walls of Jerusalem had been torn down and he wept because his heart was in Israel. The Israelites know God has promised the land of Israel to them and that their covenants through Abraham and Moses mean that Jerusalem must be established, and God should be worshipped there. Nehemiah repents for the sins of the people knowing that the destruction of the temple and walls torn down are consequences of God's people not obeying God's commandments. He intercedes for Israel. He also prays that he can get the blessing of the king on him so he can rebuild the walls. The king gives him his blessing and a letter granting authority for him to travel there.

Nehemiah 1: 4 When I heard these things, I sat down and wept. For some days I mourned and fasted and prayed before the God of heaven. 5 Then I said:

"LORD, the God of heaven, the great and awesome God, who keeps his covenant of love with those who love him and keep his commandments, 6 let your ear be attentive and your eyes open to hear the prayer your servant is praying before you day and night for your servants, the people of Israel. I confess the sins we Israelites, including myself and my father's family, have committed against you. [7] We have acted very wickedly toward you. We have not obeyed the commands, decrees and laws you gave your servant Moses.

[8] "Remember the instruction you gave your servant Moses, saying, 'If you are unfaithful, I will scatter you among the nations, [9] but if you return to me and obey my commands, then even if your exiled people are at the farthest horizon, I will gather them from there and bring them to the place I have chosen as a dwelling for my Name.'

[10] "They are your servants and your people, whom you redeemed by your great strength and your mighty hand. [11] Lord, let your ear be attentive to the prayer of this your servant and to the prayer of your servants who delight in revering your name. Give your servant success today by granting him favor in the presence of this man."

Rebuilding Jerusalem and the Temple

Nehemiah travels to Jerusalem with others. He inspects the walls himself and realizes it is a huge task. He recruits Israelis and those who accompanied him. They begin by clearing away the rubble and then placing large stones upon stones. There is resistance to their rebuilding. Enemies of Israel taunt them. They get a temporary pause in the construction by authority, but the Israelites have authority written by King Cyrus who ordered the rebuilding of the temple and paid for it. Surely, it is God's blessing on those Israelites who were living among the Gentiles who truly worshipped God and shared the truths of God within the palaces they lived in. Nehemiah and his men must work with sword in one hand and trowel in the other as there is also physical resistance to their rebuilding the walls of Jerusalem. Nehemiah remains strong and calm as he oversees the orderly construction zones by families who rebuild their sections.

    They rebuild the walls around Jerusalem and Nehemiah orders security measures. It is a tremendous victory for Israel. God used Gentile finances to rebuild the Temple. God showed his blessing on Israel by giving his people supernatural favour in the kingdoms they were scattered in. Through the rebuilding of the Temple, and rebuilding of the walls of Jerusalem, people could once more worship God. It was Israel restored. God kept His promise to Israel.

Nehemiah 7:1 After the wall had been rebuilt and I had set the doors in place, the gatekeepers, the musicians and the Levites were appointed. ²I put in charge of Jerusalem my brother Hanani, along with

Hananiah the commander of the citadel, because he was a man of integrity and feared God more than most people do. ³I said to them, "The gates of Jerusalem are not to be opened until the sun is hot. While the gatekeepers are still on duty, have them shut the doors and bar them. Also appoint residents of Jerusalem as guards, some at their posts and some near their own houses."

The walls of Jerusalem must be rebuilt so that the Israelites could be protected and rebuild their homes and their lives. The next important thing is the rebuilding of the temple. Ezra the priest oversees the start of it. He's got the official letter from King Cyrus.

Ezra 1 : ²"This is what Cyrus king of Persia says:

"'The LORD, the God of heaven, has given me all the kingdoms of the earth and he has appointed me to build a temple for him at Jerusalem in Judah. ³Any of his people among you may go up to Jerusalem in Judah and build the temple of the LORD, the God of Israel, the God who is in Jerusalem, and may their God be with them. ⁴And in any locality where survivors may now be living, the people are to provide them with silver and gold, with goods and livestock, and with freewill offerings for the temple of God in Jerusalem.'"

⁵Then the family heads of Judah and Benjamin, and the priests and Levites—everyone whose heart God had moved—prepared to go up and build the house of the LORD in Jerusalem. ⁶All their neighbors assisted them with articles of silver and gold, with goods and livestock, and with valuable gifts, in addition to all the freewill offerings.

⁷Moreover, King Cyrus brought out the articles belonging to the temple of the LORD, which Nebuchadnezzar had carried away from Jerusalem and had placed in the temple of his god.[a] ⁸Cyrus king of Persia had them brought by Mithredath the treasurer, who counted them out to Sheshbazzar the prince of Judah.

The Israelites clear away the rubble and begin laying the foundations of the temple where it had stood. There is joy and rejoicing at their victory to rebuild with authority; it is the blessing of God upon them. They respond by offering sacrifices to God to worship Him.

Ezra 3: ²Then Joshua son of Jozadak and his fellow priests and Zerubbabel son of Shealtiel and his associates began to build the altar of the God of Israel to sacrifice burnt offerings on it, in accordance with what is written in the Law of Moses the man of God. ³Despite their fear of the peoples around them, they built the altar on its foundation and sacrificed burnt offerings on it to the LORD, both the morning and evening sacrifices. ⁴Then in accordance with what is written, they celebrated the Festival of Tabernacles with the required number of burnt offerings prescribed for each day. ⁵After that, they presented the regular burnt offerings, the New Moon sacrifices and the sacrifices for all the appointed sacred festivals of the LORD, as well as those brought as freewill offerings to the LORD. ⁶On the first day of the seventh month they began to offer burnt offerings to the LORD, though the foundation of the LORD's temple had not yet been laid.

As the foundation is laid, there is more rejoicing and worship. The Israelites know it is a sign of God's covenant with them and that His presence will be with them. The Jews express their gratitude to God through celebrations, offerings, praise, worship, dancing and prayers.

Ezra 3: ¹⁰When the builders laid the foundation of the temple of the LORD, the priests in their vestments and with trumpets, and the Levites (the sons of Asaph) with cymbals, took their places to praise the LORD, as prescribed by David king of

Israel. ¹¹With praise and thanksgiving they sang to the Lord:

"He is good;
  his love toward Israel endures forever."
And all the people gave a great shout of praise to the Lord, because the foundation of the house of the Lord was laid.

After the foundations, the walls of the temple are rebuilt. There is celebration. All of Israel gathers in celebration to worship God for the miracle of rebuilding.

Ezra 6: ¹⁶Then the people of Israel—the priests, the Levites and the rest of the exiles—celebrated the dedication of the house of God with joy. ¹⁷For the dedication of this house of God they offered a hundred bulls, two hundred rams, four hundred male lambs and, as a sin offering[b] for all Israel, twelve male goats, one for each of the tribes of Israel. ¹⁸And they installed the priests in their divisions and the Levites in their groups for the service of God at Jerusalem, according to what is written in the Book of Moses.

Rebuilding of the Temple

Ezra, Nehemiah and Haggai were all part of the rebuilding of the walls and Temple of Jerusalem.

There was a reestablishment of worship and praise and Judaism. There was the reading of the Word of God once more. The Scriptures are kept by the people. Israel prospered as they obeyed God and kept his commandments. Israel flourished as the kings worshipped and praised God. As some kings departed from God, there were wars, slavery etc. Jesus was raised going to the rebuilt temple to worship. Jesus preached in that temple. The second temple was standing until 70AD when it was taken down by Rome.

The Scriptures record many attacks against Israel and as Israel was serving God, God defended them, and they were victorious. The history of the Jewish people is a record of a blessed prosperous and deeply spiritual people. As Israel did not honour God, there were attacks that prevailed. A patch of earth not large in comparison to most nations has been the focus of many countries who tried to conquer it. The miracle of Israel is in the scriptures but none the less is the miracle in the present-day resurrection of Israel after hundreds of years, in the early 1900's the people began gathering there to live once more and in 1948, it became a nation once more.

God keeps His covenants. God made covenant with Israel.

11 BOOK OF HOSEA

The Book of Hosea is an example or an allegory of God's relationship with Israel. The prophet is instructed to marry a prostitute. He does. It is symbolic of God's marriage to Israel. God compares his relationship with Israel to marrying a prostitute because of Israel's dual nature. Although God made covenant with Israel, there continued a dual nature. Sometimes Israel followed God while some kings lead Israel away from God. Gomer (the prostitute become wife) bears children. God chooses the names of the children. Jezreel, is a symbol of what God will do to the kingdom of Israel. Lo-Ruhamah is a judgment of God saying He no longer loves Israel. Lo-Ammi means Israel is no longer God's people. These are curses. These are severe judgements. The names of the children are significant. These names directly go against God's promise to cherish and keep Israel as His people. They are the consequences of Israel's sin of idolatry.

Hosea 1: ²When the LORD began to speak through Hosea, the LORD said to him, "Go, marry a promiscuous woman and have children with her, for like an adulterous wife this land is guilty of unfaithfulness to the LORD." ³So he married Gomer daughter of Diblaim, and she conceived and bore him a son.

⁴Then the LORD said to Hosea, "Call him Jezreel, because I will soon punish the house of Jehu for the massacre at Jezreel, and I will put an end to the kingdom of Israel. ⁵In that day I will break Israel's bow in the Valley of Jezreel."

⁶Gomer conceived again and gave birth to a daughter. Then the LORD said to Hosea, "Call her Lo-Ruhamah (which means "not loved"), for I will no longer show love to Israel, that I should at all forgive them. ⁷Yet I will show love to Judah; and I will save them—not by bow, sword or battle, or by horses and horsemen, but I, the LORD their God, will save them."

⁸After she had weaned Lo-Ruhamah, Gomer had another son. ⁹Then the LORD said, "Call him Lo-Ammi (which means "not my people"), for you are not my people, and I am not your God.[b]

¹⁰"Yet the Israelites will be like the sand on the seashore, which cannot be measured or counted. In the place where it was said to them, 'You are not my people,' they will be called 'children of the living God.' ¹¹The people of Judah and the people of Israel will come together; they will appoint one leader and will come up out of the land, for great will be the day of Jezreel.[c]

Even with the severe judgements there is the promise God made to Abraham the number of people as numerous as grains of sand on the seashore. The covenant is there but there is judgement because of

Israel's unfaithfulness. God directly commanded that there should be no other gods.

The book of Hosea is an allegory of God's marriage to Israel

Hosea 2: ² "Rebuke your mother, rebuke her,
　for she is not my wife,
　and I am not her husband.
Let her remove the adulterous look from her face
　and the unfaithfulness from between her breasts.
³ Otherwise I will strip her naked
　and make her as bare as on the day she was born;
I will make her like a desert,
　turn her into a parched land,
　and slay her with thirst.
⁴ I will not show my love to her children,
　because they are the children of adultery.
⁵ Their mother has been unfaithful
　and has conceived them in disgrace.
She said, 'I will go after my lovers,
　who give me my food and my water,
　my wool and my linen, my olive oil and my drink.'
⁶ Therefore I will block her path with thornbushes;

I will wall her in so that she cannot find her way.
⁷ She will chase after her lovers but not catch them;
   she will look for them but not find them.
Then she will say,
   'I will go back to my husband as at first,
   for then I was better off than now.'
⁸ She has not acknowledged that I was the one
   who gave her the grain, the new wine and oil,
who lavished on her the silver and gold—
   which they used for Baal.

      This passage is also quite harsh because of Israel's whoredoms of worshipping other gods. God will allow her to choose her way of sin, but it will be a curse to her, and she will chase after her lovers, but they will not stay with her. This describes Israeli kings making alliances with ungodly nations rather than seeking God for a solution. She will finally repent and return to her husband. It is the prophecy of Israel. It is the prophetic perception of the nation's sinning against God. She will be stripped naked and she will be out of the blessing of God. Should a person sin against God, the blessing of the covenant is no longer applied. The person will no longer succeed at anything. Baal worship included the murdering of children and sexual lewdness. It was the opposite of what God had commanded.

Hosea 2: ⁹"Therefore I will take away my grain when it ripens,
   and my new wine when it is ready.
I will take back my wool and my linen,
   intended to cover her naked body.
¹⁰ So now I will expose her lewdness
   before the eyes of her lovers;
   no one will take her out of my hands.
¹¹ I will stop all her celebrations:
   her yearly festivals, her New Moons,
   her Sabbath days—all her appointed festivals.
¹² I will ruin her vines and her fig trees,
   which she said were her pay from her lovers;
I will make them a thicket,
   and wild animals will devour them.
¹³ I will punish her for the days
   she burned incense to the Baals;
she decked herself with rings and jewelry,
   and went after her lovers,
   but me she forgot,"
declares the LORD.

    God promises to woo her back to himself so that she might once more be his cherished people. He promises that as soon as she repents, He will bless her once more. The life of plenty, abundance, peace, joy and prosperity will be hers once more. He will cherish her as His peculiar treasure or special people once more.

¹⁴ "Therefore I am now going to allure her;
   I will lead her into the wilderness
   and speak tenderly to her.
¹⁵ There I will give her back her vineyards,
   and will make the Valley of Achor[b] a door of hope.
There she will respond[c] as in the days of her youth,
   as in the day she came up out of Egypt.
¹⁶ "In that day," declares the Lord,
   "you will call me 'my husband';
   you will no longer call me 'my master.[d]'
¹⁷ I will remove the names of the Baals from her lips;
   no longer will their names be invoked.
¹⁸ In that day I will make a covenant for them
   with the beasts of the field, the birds in the sky
   and the creatures that move along the ground.
Bow and sword and battle
   I will abolish from the land,
   so that all may lie down in safety.
¹⁹ I will betroth you to me forever;
   I will betroth you in[e] righteousness and justice,
   in[f] love and compassion.
²⁰ I will betroth you in[g] faithfulness,
   and you will acknowledge the Lord.

The blessings will be as though she never had sinned. God's special blessing of Israel shall be my people and He will be their God will be upon her. Life in covenant with God, is the only life worth living because there is joy, peace, protection, Divine protection and supernatural provision and blessing.

²¹ "In that day I will respond,"
    declares the LORD—
"I will respond to the skies,
    and they will respond to the earth;
²² and the earth will respond to the grain,
    the new wine and the olive oil,
    and they will respond to Jezreel.[h]
²³ I will plant her for myself in the land;
    I will show my love to the one I called 'Not my loved one.[i]'
I will say to those called 'Not my people,[j]' 'You are my people';
    and they will say, 'You are my God.'"

Hosea the prophet lived this situation. Often prophets in the Old Covenant or Mosaic covenant physically experienced things that were a sign to Israel. In this instance, Hosea's wife runs off and becomes a prostitute once more until she is sold into slavery, naked with other slaves. He reclaims her by purchasing her, taking her home. He leaves her alone for a season and then cherishes her as his wife once more. Hosea's life is written as an allegory of God's relationship with Israel and His patient desire for her to repent and return to Him. It is grace or unmerited love that God shows to Israel. Although this scripture applies to Israel, it can also apply to any Christian who repents and lives his life wholly for God once more.

12 MALICHI

Some of the prophets in the Old Covenant directly prophesy against Israel and her wicked kings. They spoke to kings, experienced persecution for their words because they warned the kings to return to God.

The prophet Malachi warned people to serve God giving the tithes and offerings. This was part of the covenant God made with Moses. There should be a tenth of the income given to God. It meant bringing in sheep or oxen or grain or money. God had promised to bless Israel for doing it. In not keeping this commandment, it meant that the Levites who have no other source of income, were not properly cared for and couldn't do their regular duties in ministry. The offering of the tithe means the protection and blessing of God on the giver.

Malachi 3: 6"I the LORD do not change. So you, the descendants of Jacob, are not destroyed. 7 Ever since the time of your ancestors you have turned away from my decrees and have not kept them. Return to me, and I will return to you," says the LORD Almighty.

"But you ask, 'How are we to return?'

8"Will a mere mortal rob God? Yet you rob me.

"But you ask, 'How are we robbing you?'

"In tithes and offerings. [9] You are under a curse—your whole nation—because you are robbing me. [10] Bring the whole tithe into the storehouse, that there may be food in my house. Test me in this," says the LORD Almighty, "and see if I will not throw open the floodgates of heaven and pour out so much blessing that there will not be room enough to store it. [11] I will prevent pests from devouring your crops, and the vines in your fields will not drop their fruit before it is ripe," says the LORD Almighty. [12] "Then all the nations will call you blessed, for yours will be a delightful land," says the LORD Almighty.

After the book of Malachi, there were 400 years of darkness for the nation of Israel. No prophets are recorded. It was God's silence as Israel the nation was not serving Him.

13 GOD'S SPECIAL MERCY ON ISRAEL

God chose Israel as he chose Abraham and made covenant with him. The blessings of Abraham not only apply to his family but all of Israel. They apply to believers in Christ because the blessings of Abraham are ours by faith. God will bless those who bless Israel and curse those who curse Israel.

Blessing on Abraham

Genesis 12: 2 "I will make you into a great nation,
   and I will bless you;
I will make your name great,
   and you will be a blessing.[a]
3 I will bless those who bless you,
   and whoever curses you I will curse;
and all peoples on earth
   will be blessed through you."[b]

Moses and Joshua brought the nation of Israel to possess the land promised to Abraham – Canaan. The land that is Israel was a special gift to the nation of Israel, but it is essential to Christians to honour Israel and pray for her because God has made covenant with Israel. There is historical significance in Israel. There is archeological evidence of scriptural truths being discovered regularly. There is much prophecy concerning Israel in the Scriptures.

Worshippers and ark of covenant would be first in battle – The kings of Israel brought the ark of the covenant with him into battle because the strength of Israel is the God of Israel.

God defends Israel by supernatural means –

100, 000 slain by an angel

God delivered Israel from the Assyrian army that threatened Israel and mocked God. One angel came and delivered all of Israel.

2 Kings 19: **35 That night the angel of the L**ORD **went out and put to death a hundred and eighty-five thousand in the Assyrian camp. When the people got up the next morning—there were all the dead bodies! 36 So Sennacherib king of Assyria broke camp and withdrew. He returned to Nineveh and stayed there.**

Sound of lepers scared off the enemy – spared Jerusalem

The Arameans surrounded Israel and there was no food or water in Israel. The lepers who were dying marched towards the enemy camp. They took a step of faith to save themselves rather than die. God magnified the sound of their steps so that it sounded like thousands of troops and scared off the enemy army.

2 Kings 7: 3 Now there were four men with leprosy[d] at the entrance of the city gate. They said to each other, "Why stay here until we die? 4 If we say, 'We'll go into the city'—the famine is there, and we will die. And if we stay here, we will die. So let's go over to the camp of the Arameans and surrender. If they spare us, we live; if they kill us, then we die."

5 At dusk they got up and went to the camp of the Arameans. When they reached the edge of the camp, no one was there, 6 for the Lord had caused the Arameans to hear the sound of chariots and horses and a great army, so that they said to one another, "Look, the king of Israel has hired the Hittite and Egyptian kings to attack us!" 7 So they got up and fled in the dusk and abandoned their tents and their horses and donkeys. They left the camp as it was and ran for their lives.

8 The men who had leprosy reached the edge of the camp, entered one of the tents and ate and drank. Then they took silver, gold and clothes, and went off and hid them. They returned and entered another tent and took some things from it and hid them also.

⁹Then they said to each other, "What we're doing is not right. This is a day of good news and we are keeping it to ourselves. If we wait until daylight, punishment will overtake us. Let's go at once and report this to the royal palace."

God made the water seem as if blood and scared off enemy

The Moabites were attacking Israel and Judah. The prophet Elisha instructed the kings what to do. They dug trenches and filled them with water. The sun shone on those trenches and it appeared to the enemy as blood. They were frightened and ran off killing each other.

2 Kings 3: While the harpist was playing, the hand of the LORD came on Elisha ¹⁶and he said, "This is what the LORD says: I will fill this valley with pools of water. ¹⁷For this is what the LORD says: You will see neither wind nor rain, yet this valley will be filled with water, and you, your cattle and your other animals will drink. ¹⁸This is an easy thing in the eyes of the LORD; he will also deliver Moab into your hands. ¹⁹You will overthrow every fortified city and every major town. You will cut down every good tree, stop up all the springs, and ruin every good field with stones."

²⁰The next morning, about the time for offering the sacrifice, there it was—water flowing from the

direction of Edom! And the land was filled with water.

²¹ Now all the Moabites had heard that the kings had come to fight against them; so every man, young and old, who could bear arms was called up and stationed on the border. ²² When they got up early in the morning, the sun was shining on the water. To the Moabites across the way, the water looked red—like blood. ²³ "That's blood!" they said. "Those kings must have fought and slaughtered each other. Now to the plunder, Moab!"

²⁴ But when the Moabites came to the camp of Israel, the Israelites rose up and fought them until they fled. And the Israelites invaded the land and slaughtered the Moabites. ²⁵ They destroyed the towns, and each man threw a stone on every good field until it was covered. They stopped up all the springs and cut down every good tree. Only Kir Hareseth was left with its stones in place, but men armed with slings surrounded it and attacked it.

God judges those who fight against Israel and deals roughly with them

God severely punishes those who fight against Israel. This is the Abrahamic covenant. It is also the Mosaic covenant. The Prophet Isaiah records judgements upon those who fight against Israel and abuse her.

Isaiah 47: ⁶I was angry with my people
  and desecrated my inheritance;
I gave them into your hand,
  and you showed them no mercy.
Even on the aged
  you laid a very heavy yoke.
⁷You said, 'I am forever—
  the eternal queen!'
But you did not consider these things
  or reflect on what might happen.
⁸"Now then, listen, you lover of pleasure,
  lounging in your security
and saying to yourself,
  'I am, and there is none besides me.
I will never be a widow
  or suffer the loss of children.'
⁹Both of these will overtake you
  in a moment, on a single day:
  loss of children and widowhood.
They will come upon you in full measure,
  in spite of your many sorceries
  and all your potent spells.
¹⁰You have trusted in your wickedness
  and have said, 'No one sees me.'
Your wisdom and knowledge mislead you
  when you say to yourself,
  'I am, and there is none besides me.'
¹¹Disaster will come upon you,

and you will not know how to conjure it away.

Those who opposed Israel or abused her were destroyed.

    The Babylonians fought against Israel, and but they did not prevail as a people the end of the Babylonian Empire   587 BC.
The Roman Empire fought against Israel, but the end of the Roman Empire was 476 AD.

    In the Last war – all nations that rise against Israel will be destroyed at Armageddon. It will be the end of earth as we know it the final judgement.

14 JESUS THE MESSIAH

There was always a remnant of Jews who served God. Some of them had to do it privately because of the wickedness of the kings. The hope of a Messiah, a deliverer was spoken in Genesis 3. As soon as Adam and Eve sinned, there was the promise of one of the woman's children that would rise to crush the head of the serpent. The book of Isaiah specifically foretells the coming of the Messiah and gives prophetic scriptures concerning His coming. Other books of the Old Covenant also point to the Messiah. Marilyn Hickey, an American preacher, evangelist, has got a book on Jesus in every book on the Bible. Jesus Christ is prophesied of in the Old Covenant and is the centre of the New Covenant.

John the Baptist was preaching during Jesus life. They were approximately the same age. John the Baptist was a prophet who was preaching in the wilderness so crowds could gather to hear him. He baptised people who committed their lives to Christ. His main message was to repent – receive God and expect the Messiah to come. Thousands of people would gather because he was speaking for God.

Jesus was born of the virgin Mary. His birth was miraculous. God sovereignly placed Jesus within her womb. Joseph married her after he was given an angelic dream that told him to. They raised Jesus as an ordinary child although they both knew he was not just an ordinary child. Joseph and Mary both experienced angelic visitations and miraculous signs regarding Jesus birth. They received prophecies over Jesus at the Temple at his circumcision. They were both believing Jews and they raised Jesus with a life of prayer, praise, worship, sacrifice keeping the covenant with Moses.

Luke 2: [41] Every year Jesus' parents went to Jerusalem for the Festival of the Passover. [42] When he was twelve years old, they went up to the festival, according to the custom. [43] After the festival was over, while his parents were returning home, the boy Jesus stayed behind in Jerusalem, but they were unaware of it. [44] Thinking he was in their company, they traveled on for a day. Then they began looking for him among their relatives and friends. [45] When they did not find him, they went back to Jerusalem to look for him. [46] After three days they found him in the temple courts, sitting among the teachers, listening to them and asking them questions. [47] Everyone who heard him was amazed at his understanding and his answers. [48] When his parents saw him, they were astonished. His mother said to him, "Son, why have you treated us like this? Your father and I have been anxiously searching for you."

⁴⁹ "Why were you searching for me?" he asked. "Didn't you know I had to be in my Father's house?"[t] ⁵⁰ But they did not understand what he was saying to them.

Even as a child, he was interested in speaking of the things of God and the scriptures. Jesus lived mostly an ordinary life as a carpenter until age 30. From ages 30-33 he had a ministry of miracles, signs, wonders, preaching, teaching. He was baptized by John the Baptist and John the Baptist, prophesied over him saying Jesus was the lamb of God who would take the sins of the world away (John 1: 29).

Israel is essential to Christianity because Jesus who fulfilled all Messianic prophecy suffered and died on the cross and rose from the dead and ascended into heaven. Jesus was a devout Jew all his life. He taught the Scriptures in a way ordinary people could understand.

Jesus -fulfilled God's Torah, laws and they apply to us through Jesus Christ – our Saviour – the Messiah

Jesus announced He was the Lord of the sabbath. This means He is equal to God who gave the commandments. This means it is essential to embrace Christ as Saviour, as LORD. Jesus is the Messiah.

Matthew 12: ⁶I tell you that something greater than the temple is here. ⁷If you had known what these words mean, 'I desire mercy, not sacrifice,'[a] you would not have condemned the innocent. ⁸For the Son of Man is Lord of the Sabbath."

Jesus is the Word of God. The Holy Scriptures were inspired by the Holy Spirit. They are written by the Holy Spirit through godly men. Jesus is the inspired Word of God.

John 1:1 In the beginning was the Word, and the Word was with God, and the Word was God. ²He was with God in the beginning. ³Through him all things were made; without him nothing was made that has been made.⁴ In him was life, and that life was the light of all mankind. ⁵The light shines in the darkness, and the darkness has not overcome[a] it.

Jesus is man. He was born of the virgin Mary. He has a physical human male body. He lives in this resurrected body. The wounds through his hands and feet are visible. The Son of God became human. He remained God and human simultaneously. Now in his glorified body, his resurrected body, he appears as a human but with the glory of God shinning through him. We will recognize him by the scars in his body.

John 1: ¹⁴The Word became flesh and made his dwelling among us. We have seen his glory, the glory of the one and only Son, who came from the Father, full of grace and truth.

Jesus fulfilled all Messianic prophecies concerning himself in the Scriptures. Jesus said he did not come to ignore the law or to end it but to fulfill it. He met all the requirements of the law as a sacrifice to atone for all sin. Only God could do it. Jesus is God. He surrendered his life as a wholly spotless lamb. He died so that all who believe in him could be saved: cleansed from all sin, healed, delivered and live in peace with God once more.

Matthew 5: ¹⁷"Do not think that I have come to abolish the Law or the Prophets; I have not come to abolish them but to fulfill them. ¹⁸For truly I tell you, until heaven and earth disappear, not the smallest letter, not the least stroke of a pen, will by any means disappear from the Law until everything is accomplished. ¹⁹Therefore anyone who sets aside one of the least of these commands and teaches others accordingly will be called least in the kingdom of heaven, but whoever practices and teaches these commands will be called great in the kingdom of heaven.

Our Saviour is a Jew. He is not just any Jew, but he never sinned. He lived a holy life and he declared Himself that He was the Son of God. All who believe on Jesus – that he died for our sins and rose form the dead will be saved.

Romans 10: ¹³ for, "Everyone who calls on the name of the Lord will be saved."[f]

All the disciples, the first Apostles, were Jews. Gentiles can only come to God – all people can only be saved through Jesus Christ.

John 14: ⁶ Jesus answered, "I am the way and the truth and the life. No one comes to the Father except through me."

Jesus fulfilled all the laws of the covenant of Moses and made a way for not only Jews but Gentiles to be saved. This is a miracle because we Gentiles are not descendants of the covenant of Moses. There would be no hope for us except through Jesus Christ.

Galatians 3: ²⁸ There is neither Jew nor Gentile, neither slave nor free, nor is there male and female, for you are all one in Christ Jesus.

Through Jesus Christ came salvation of the Jews and Gentiles. But God's covenant with Israel remains. Not all the Jewish people accepted Christ. Some did but some did not. Now, there are some Jewish believers in Jesus the Messiah. Many do not yet know Him, but a day will surely come when they do. The Apostle Paul speaks of this directly. He compares it to a natural branch of an olive tree being re grafted into the tree it came from.

Romans 11: [11]Again I ask: Did they stumble so as to fall beyond recovery? Not at all! Rather, because of their transgression, salvation has come to the Gentiles to make Israel envious. [12]But if their transgression means riches for the world, and their loss means riches for the Gentiles, how much greater riches will their full inclusion bring!

[13]I am talking to you Gentiles. Inasmuch as I am the apostle to the Gentiles, I take pride in my ministry [14]in the hope that I may somehow arouse my own people to envy and save some of them. [15]For if their rejection brought reconciliation to the world, what will their acceptance be but life from the dead? [16]If the part of the dough offered as firstfruits is holy, then the whole batch is holy; if the root is holy, so are the branches.

[25]I do not want you to be ignorant of this mystery, brothers and sisters, so that you may not be

conceited: Israel has experienced a hardening in part until the full number of the Gentiles has come in, [26] and in this way[e] all Israel will be saved.

Through Jesus Christ, Jews and Gentiles are knit together as one people. We are all worshippers of Messiah. This should be the longing of every Christian and Messianic Christian. Gentiles were idol worshippers without hope of salvation. Jesus and the message of the gospel, his death, burial and resurrection spread throughout the earth and with it, multitudes of Gentiles or non-Jews have become Christians. Followers of Jesus Christ inherit the blessings of Abraham, Isaac and Jacob. The promises of God belong to us because Jesus fulfilled all prophecy and promised us that anyone who believed in him would never die. Jews who did not receive Jesus as he first came to earth because they did not know him to be the Messiah shall be once more grafted in to the olive tree or the seed of Abraham – with all the blessings of the Old covenant with Moses and all the blessings of the New Covenant with Jesus. We shall be one people who worship God truly in Spirit and in truth.

15 JESUS IS THE LIVING WORD OF GOD

Jesus is the Son of God, equal with God. Christians believe that Jesus is God – one with God and the Holy Spirit – a trinity. The book of John describes this in the words of Jesus is the Word of God and became flesh. Jesus is eternal. He is the Son of God, but He is also existing with God and equal to God but distinct in expression as is the Holy Spirit. The three are one. They have distinct expressions. As water can be liquid or frozen into ice or boiled into steam – they are all water but distinct in expression. Jesus is the Word of God. The Word of God was inspired by the Holy Spirit. The Word of God came directly from God. The Holy Scriptures are God's words to us for how to live life on earth so that we can live in the blessing of His covenants with us. They are directions for living. Jesus is the Word of God. He is the inspired Word of God equal with the Holy Spirit and God.

John 1: [14] **The Word became flesh and made his dwelling among us. We have seen his glory, the glory of the one and only Son, who came from the Father, full of grace and truth.**

Jesus himself explained there is no other Messiah but him. There is only one way to Salvation, it is believing on the LORD Jesus Christ. Jesus Messiah is the only hope for people to live without sin. Through faith in Jesus Christ, the sin of Adam is blotted out. Jesus blood accomplished it. Only the blood of a human without sin could ransom the lives of humans with sin. All of us born of Adam are sinners because the sin of Adam is in our heritage. Jesus mother was Mary. Joseph raised Jesus as his own son, but it was the Holy Spirit that came upon Mary so that she conceived. No sin in Jesus bloodline because God is the essence of Jesus. Jesus is the only way. No other person could live holy – only God himself could be a sacrifice worthy to atone for human sin. Jesus is the hope for Jew and Gentile.

John 14: [6] Jesus answered, "I am the way and the truth and the life. No one comes to the Father except through me.

Jesus told his disciples He was the light of the world. He brought revelation of God through his life. As the prophets were examples to Israel so is Jesus the ultimate example to Israel and all of us. Jesus knew he was going to die and be resurrected. He hinted at it and plainly told his disciples in some scriptures.

John 12: [35] Then Jesus told them, "You are going to have the light just a little while longer. Walk while you have the light, before darkness overtakes you. Whoever walks in the dark does not know where they are going.[36] Believe in the light while you have the light, so that you may become children of light." When he had finished speaking, Jesus left and hid himself from them.

Through Jesus Christ there is salvation. It means there is forgiveness of sins. It means Jesus was as the sacrifice to atone for our sins, but He is the ultimate sacrifice - the sinless Son of God who offered Himself as penalty for all sins of all people should they believe on him. Through Jesus Christ, we Gentiles have the blessings of Abraham and the covenant of Moses because Jesus fulfilled the requirements for all of them.

We who receive Christ have the Spirit of God dwelling within us. We are made one by the Holy Spirit. We believers corporately are the Church of Jesus Christ.

Galatians 3: [26] So in Christ Jesus you are all children of God through faith, [27] for all of you who were baptized into Christ have clothed yourselves with Christ. [28] There is neither Jew nor Gentile, neither slave nor free, nor is there male and female, for you are all one in Christ Jesus. [29] If you belong to Christ, then you are Abraham's seed, and heirs according to the promise.

Jesus did not send the law – he fulfilled it through his life death burial and resurrection. Jesus promised to return. He said he would prepare a place for is. It is not necessarily only a location but a destination – eternal salvation.

John 14: ³And if I go and prepare a place for you, I will come back and take you to be with me that you also may be where I am.

He was a devout practising Jew – but he was different from all other people because he never sinned – John the Baptist prophesied over him as the lamb of God. God the Baptist saw the Holy Spirit descend upon him as a dove. He heard God say that Jesus is His Son.

John 1: ²⁹The next day John saw Jesus coming toward him and said, "Look, the Lamb of God, who takes away the sin of the world! ³⁰This is the one I meant when I said, 'A man who comes after me has surpassed me because he was before me.' ³¹I myself did not know him, but the reason I came baptizing with water was that he might be revealed to Israel."
³²Then John gave this testimony: "I saw the Spirit come down from heaven as a dove and remain on him. ³³And I myself did not know him, but the one who sent me to baptize with

water told me, 'The man on whom you see the Spirit come down and remain is the one who will baptize with the Holy Spirit.' ³⁴ I have seen and I testify that this is God's Chosen One."[f]

Jesus earthly ministry was preaching and teaching the truths of the Old Covenant scriptures so that ordinary people could comprehend them. He taught the scriptures with authority because He is one with the Holy Spirit – the author of the Scriptures. He would preach in the temple until the jealous angry Jewish leaders tried to kill him.

John 11: ⁴⁷ Then the chief priests and the Pharisees called a meeting of the Sanhedrin.

"What are we accomplishing?" they asked. "Here is this man performing many signs. ⁴⁸ If we let him go on like this, everyone will believe in him, and then the Romans will come and take away both our temple and our nation."

⁴⁹ Then one of them, named Caiaphas, who was high priest that year, spoke up, "You know nothing at all! ⁵⁰ You do not realize that it is better for you that one man die for the people than that the whole nation perish."

⁵¹ He did not say this on his own, but as high priest that year he prophesied that Jesus would die for the

Jewish nation, ⁵²and not only for that nation but also for the scattered children of God, to bring them together and make them one. ⁵³So from that day on they plotted to take his life.

⁵⁴Therefore Jesus no longer moved about publicly among the people of Judea. Instead he withdrew to a region near the wilderness, to a village called Ephraim, where he stayed with his disciples.

Jesus fulfilled the Messianic prophecies. This passage describes the Messiah giving his life for his people. It is a description of Jesus being beaten and suffering in place of us. He took upon himself all our punishments and judgements so that should we repent believing in Jesus, He would cleanse us from all sin.

Isaiah prophesied the coming of Messiah

In the book of Isaiah is the prophecy of Jesus birth, death and mission. Jesus is from the lineage of David. He is from the Tribe of Judah. He is described as a mighty God, the prince of peace. He is prophesied to reign on the throne of David – meaning he should reign in Jerusalem.

Isaiah 9: ⁶For to us a child is born,
   to us a son is given,
   and the government will be on his shoulders.

And he will be called
   Wonderful Counselor, Mighty God,
   Everlasting Father, Prince of Peace.
⁷Of the greatness of his government and peace
   there will be no end.
He will reign on David's throne
   and over his kingdom,
establishing and upholding it
   with justice and righteousness
   from that time on and forever.
The zeal of the LORD Almighty
   will accomplish this.

The suffering of the Messiah is described in Isaiah 53. It includes his suffering beating and death for the sins of the people. Jesus fulfilled all these things as he was falsely accused, judged and condemned to die with sinners even though he himself committed no sin. It includes his burial with the rich as his uncle Joseph of Arimathea gave his burial chamber to be used for Jesus. Each of these prophecies were fulfilled as written in the gospels of Matthew, Mark, Luke and John.

Isaiah 53: ²He grew up before him like a tender shoot,
   and like a root out of dry ground.
He had no beauty or majesty to attract us to him,
   nothing in his appearance that we should desire

him.
³ He was despised and rejected by mankind,
   a man of suffering, and familiar with pain.
Like one from whom people hide their faces
   he was despised, and we held him in low esteem.
⁴ Surely he took up our pain
   and bore our suffering,
yet we considered him punished by God,
   stricken by him, and afflicted.
⁵ But he was pierced for our transgressions,
   he was crushed for our iniquities;
the punishment that brought us peace was on him,
   and by his wounds we are healed.
⁶ We all, like sheep, have gone astray,
   each of us has turned to our own way;
and the LORD has laid on him
   the iniquity of us all.
⁷ He was oppressed and afflicted,
   yet he did not open his mouth;
he was led like a lamb to the slaughter,
   and as a sheep before its shearers is silent,
   so he did not open his mouth.
⁸ By oppression[a] and judgment he was taken away.
   Yet who of his generation protested?
For he was cut off from the land of the living;
   for the transgression of my people he was punished.[b]
⁹ He was assigned a grave with the wicked,
   and with the rich in his death,

though he had done no violence,
    nor was any deceit in his mouth.
¹⁰ Yet it was the LORD's will to crush him and cause him to suffer,
    and though the LORD makes[c] his life an offering for sin,
he will see his offspring and prolong his days,
    and the will of the LORD will prosper in his hand.
¹¹ After he has suffered,
    he will see the light of life[d] and be satisfied[e];
by his knowledge[f] my righteous servant will justify many,
    and he will bear their iniquities.
¹² Therefore I will give him a portion among the great,[g]
    and he will divide the spoils with the strong,[h]
because he poured out his life unto death,
    and was numbered with the transgressors.
For he bore the sin of many,
    and made intercession for the transgressors.

The ultimate summary of these scriptures can be traced to all new covenant scriptures. Jesus lived all these verses. Jesus willingly gave his life for all who would believe in him as the sacrifice for sin. Sinless man, equal with God, was slain – a willing sacrifice to atone for the sins of humans who have no other way to achieve peace with God. Jesus, the lamb of God, pure, without sin, willingly shed his blood so that we who believe in him might live forever.

Ministry of Messiah

Jesus ministry on the earth can be described in Isaiah's prophecy in Isaiah 61. Jesus is Saviour of our souls. Jesus is Healer. Jesus is a Deliverer. Jesus is life. There is nothing that Jesus cannot do. The good news is that through Jesus Christ humans can be free from sin. We can have communion with God. We can speak with Him and He dwells within us. Jesus healed the sick. Jesus raised the dead. Jesus cast our demons. Jesus set people free. His preaching brought hope to people and understanding of God. His message brought life to the scriptures because He was living the Word of God. He truly loved people with unconditional love. Often, he was moved with compassion and healed someone.

Isaiah 61:1 The Spirit of the Sovereign LORD is on me,
    because the LORD has anointed me
    to proclaim good news to the poor.
He has sent me to bind up the broken hearted,
    to proclaim freedom for the captives
    and release from darkness for the prisoners,[a]
2 to proclaim the year of the LORD's favor

and the day of vengeance of our God,
to comfort all who mourn,
3 and provide for those who grieve in Zion—
to bestow on them a crown of beauty
    instead of ashes,
the oil of joy
    instead of mourning,
and a garment of praise
    instead of a spirit of despair.
They will be called oaks of righteousness,
    a planting of the LORD
    for the display of his splendor.

Only through Christ can we fully come wholly to God – He sacrificed his blood so we could have eternal life. The Holy Spirit dwells in us giving us the fruit of the Holy Spirit or the character of God. The Holy Spirit lives inside of believers. As we obey the promptings of the Holy Spirit, God uses us in the ministry of preaching and sharing the good news of Jesus. We who obey God's commandments to preach the gospel preach Salvation, Healing, Deliverance and abundance through Jesus Christ. It can only come by faith.

Galatians 5: 22 But the fruit of the Spirit is love, joy, peace, forbearance, kindness, goodness, faithfulness, 23 gentleness and self-control. Against such things there is no law.

1 John 3: ⁵But you know that he appeared so that he might take away our sins. And in him is no sin.

Jesus blood replaced the animal sacrifices of the Mosaic covenant. No longer are they required. It is necessary that we believe on Jesus blood as our redemption. He died once and for all. There is no other sacrifice necessary because He fulfilled all the requirements of the law and kept the covenant of Moses without sin.

Hebrews 9: ¹³The blood of goats and bulls and the ashes of a heifer sprinkled on those who are ceremonially unclean sanctify them so that they are outwardly clean. ¹⁴How much more, then, will the blood of Christ, who through the eternal Spirit offered himself unblemished to God, cleanse our consciences from acts that lead to death,[c] so that we may serve the living God!

Jesus words to his disciples when he rose from the dead was to preach the good news of Jesus death, burial and resurrection offering hope of salvation to all who would believe on him. Jesus would live inside of those believer's who accept him in the person of the Holy Spirit. God Himself dwelling inside of us. Rather than in a place such as a temple, as glorious as it was, God dwells within the believer in Christ.

Col 1: ²⁷ To them God has chosen to make known among the Gentiles the glorious riches of this mystery, which is Christ in you, the hope of glory.

The Baptism of Holy Spirit was upon the 120 Jewish disciples who gathered in Jerusalem on the day of Pentecost. They were filled to overflowing with the Holy Spirit so that they spoke in other tongues. Some of them spoke in languages they had never learned. The baptism of the Holy Spirit was given to empower them to preach the gospel of Jesus Christ in Jerusalem, Judea, Samaria and the uttermost parts of the world. The disciples did not have modern travel means. They used what they had. They did not have microphones or convention centers yet through them the good news of Jesus has spread throughout most of the earth. There are millions of believing Christians.

Acts 1: ⁸ But you will receive power when the Holy Spirit comes on you; and you will be my witnesses in Jerusalem, and in all Judea and Samaria, and to the ends of the earth."

The commandment to preach the gospel is known as the great commission. It is necessary for all Christians to share their faith with those who are in their lives. Some people preach in ministry as missionaries or ministers. Many of the congregational members share Christ one on one. It is necessary that we reach all people groups and nationalities and ethnicities. God wants all people to know Jesus is their Saviour.

Matthew 24: 14 And this gospel of the kingdom will be preached in the whole world as a testimony to all nations, and then the end will come.

On earth, true worshippers of God started with Israel because God chose Israel. believers started with Israel. The final last war will be against Israel and end in Israel. It will be the end of the age or of the earth as we know it. Israel is essential because Jesus will return to Israel once more. He promised to return. He will establish his throne at Jerusalem in the rebuilt temple. He will reign on earth with all believers in him for a thousand years. Jesus return to earth will be visible. He will come from the skies in the same manner that he ascended into heaven at the mount of Olives.

Acts 1: 11 "Men of Galilee," they said, "why do you stand here looking into the sky? This same Jesus, who has been taken from you into heaven, will come back in the same way you have seen him go into heaven."

Revelation 1: [7]"Look, he is coming with the clouds,"[b]
   and "every eye will see him,
even those who pierced him";
   and all peoples on earth "will mourn because of him."[c]
So shall it be! Amen.
[8]"I am the Alpha and the Omega," says the Lord God, "who is, and who was, and who is to come, the Almighty."

Israel our Christian Heritage: Israel our Christian Destiny

16 THE THIRD TEMPLE PROPHECY

Israel is important to the church because Jesus will reign on the earth for a thousand years from his throne in the rebuilt temple at Jerusalem. The rebuilding of the Jewish Temple is controversial because Christians, Jews and Muslims consider the Temple Mound a Holy place. It seems it is impossible that the Jews can rebuild a temple there because of the claims of the other groups. There are Old Covenant prophesies of the rebuilding of the temple. There is promise for the rebuilding of the temple at Jerusalem. Also, it is in the prophesied in the book of Revelation that Jesus will reign for a thousand years from the Temple at Jerusalem.

Revelation 20: 4 I saw thrones on which were seated those who had been given authority to judge. And I saw the souls of those who had been beheaded because of their testimony about Jesus and because of the word of God. They[a] had not worshiped the beast or its image and had not received its mark on their foreheads or their hands. They came to life and reigned with Christ a thousand years. 5 (The rest of the dead did not come to life until the thousand years were ended.) This is the first resurrection. [6] Blessed and holy are those who share in the first resurrection. The second death has no power over them, but they will be priests of God and of Christ and will reign with him for a thousand years.

Jesus compares himself to the temple

Jesus himself compared his own death, burial and resurrection to the destruction of the temple and rebuilding of it. The temple is important as it is the dwelling place of God. God's presence first was upon people in the presence of the Holy Spirit with the anointing – God's Spirit would come upon a person. Later, Moses built the Tabernacle in the wilderness according to God's commandments. It was the dwelling of place of God with Israel. The temple became a place of worship, praise, sacrifice and gathering for the people of Jerusalem once it was built in Jerusalem. God's Holy presence was in the ark of the covenant. His glory cloud filled the temple. After Jesus death, burial and resurrection, Jesus breathed on the disciples and said "Receive the Holy Spirit" It was God's gift as promised. It was the presence of God dwelling within those who believed in Christ. The day of Pentecost brought the Baptism of the Holy Spirit where the Spirit's presence was so overwhelming that the people were worshipping God in tongues. They were empowered to preach the gospel throughout the earth.

Jesus will reign on earth in the rebuilt temple at Jerusalem. There will be Jews and Gentiles together as Christians worshipping Messiah. There will be no sacrifices because Jesus life was the ultimate sacrifice. Jesus compares Himself to the temple. It is the prophecy of his death, burial and resurrection. He is identifying with the temple, the place of worship – the indwelling presence of God in him.

John 2: [18] The Jews then responded to him, "What sign can you show us to prove your authority to do all this?"

[19] Jesus answered them, "Destroy this temple, and I will raise it again in three days."

[20] They replied, "It has taken forty-six years to build this temple, and you are going to raise it in three days?" [21] But the temple he had spoken of was his body. [22] After he was raised from the dead, his disciples recalled what he had said. Then they believed the scripture and the words that Jesus had spoken.

Jesus prophesies over the 2nd temple that a day will come when it will no longer be standing. It occurred in 70 AD. It also applies to himself as he was crucified, died and rose on the third day.

Matthew 24:1 Jesus left the temple and was walking away when his disciples came up to him to call his attention to its buildings. ²"Do you see all these things?" he asked. "Truly I tell you, not one stone here will be left on another; everyone will be thrown down."

³As Jesus was sitting on the Mount of Olives, the disciples came to him privately. "Tell us," they said, "when will this happen, and what will be the sign of your coming and of the end of the age?"

The prophecy over the ruler who will crown himself as Messiah – the antichrist

The prophecy of the rebuilding of the temple is in Daniel. The rebuilding occurs before Jesus returns to earth to reign. First the antichrist (the devil) will proclaim himself as god there. Many people will be deceived by him – he will claim to be the Messiah and bring peace on the earth for three and a half years. Because it is not earthly possible to bring peace on earth, many people will believe he is the Messiah. Only those who truly know God will not be deceived. Jesus the Messiah shed his blood so that there is no more sacrifice necessary. Animal sacrifices are not to be re established because Jesus blood is the sacrifice for all people.

Daniel 9: ²⁴"Seventy 'sevens'[c] are decreed for your people and your holy city to finish[d] transgression, to put an end to sin, to atone for wickedness, to bring in everlasting righteousness, to seal up vision and prophecy and to anoint the Most Holy Place.[e]

25 "Know and understand this: From the time the word goes out to restore and rebuild Jerusalem until the Anointed One,[f] the ruler, comes, there will be seven 'sevens,' and sixty-two 'sevens.' It will be rebuilt with streets and a trench, but in times of trouble. 26 After the sixty-two 'sevens,' the Anointed One will be put to death and will have nothing.[g] The people of the ruler who will come will destroy the city and the sanctuary. The end will come like a flood: War will continue until the end, and desolations have been decreed. 27 He will confirm a covenant with many for one 'seven.'[h] In the middle of the 'seven'[i] he will put an end to sacrifice and offering. And at the temple[j] he will set up an abomination that causes desolation, until the end that is decreed is poured out on him.[k]"[l]

Matthew 24: 15 "So when you see standing in the holy place 'the abomination that causes desolation,'[a] spoken of through the prophet Daniel—let the reader understand—

    Jesus will return to the earth and everyone will see him. He is in his resurrected body so the wounds in his hands and feet are visible. Most of the Jewish people will accept Him as He appears. There will be multitudes coming to Christ as He comes to earth. He will come and reign on the earth as Messiah in the temple at Jerusalem and a thousand years of peace will follow.

17 THE 2ND COMING OF JESUS CHRIST

Jesus will return to earth– reign in the Temple in Jerusalem for 1,000 years; these will be years of peace and prosperity. During those years, believers shall experience heaven on earth because the devil will be bound for the duration and there will be no evil. Not all people on earth will be believers. God will not force His kingdom on anyone. Many Jewish people will come to Christ because they will recognize him by the nail prints in his hands and feet and they will receive him as Messiah. This will be the fulfillment of the prayer of the Apostle Paul that all of Israel will be saved. They shall look on him whom they have pierced and mourn for him.

God promised He would graft Israel into God's side once more – Apostle Paul – all of Israel shall be saved. Although Israel did not accept Jesus as Messiah at his first coming, they will receive Him as Messiah. It is God's promise. The olive tree is a symbol of Israel. It is known for its beauty and its fruit. The Gentiles or non-Jews who believed in Jesus – Christians – have been grafted into Israel. We shall inherit the promises of Abraham by faith, of Moses by faith – in Jesus Christ the Messiah.

Romans 11: ⁱ⁷ If some of the branches have been broken off, and you, though a wild olive shoot, have been grafted in among the others and now share in the nourishing sap from the olive root, ¹⁸ do not consider yourself to be superior to those other branches. If you do, consider this: You do not support the root, but the root supports you. ¹⁹ You will say then, "Branches were broken off so that I could be grafted in."

²³ And if they do not persist in unbelief, they will be grafted in, for God is able to graft them in again. ²⁴ After all, if you were cut out of an olive tree that is wild by nature, and contrary to nature were grafted into a cultivated olive tree, how much more readily will these, the natural branches, be grafted into their own olive tree!

Romans 11: ²⁵ I do not want you to be ignorant of this mystery, brothers and sisters, so that you may not be conceited: Israel has experienced a hardening in part until the full number of the Gentiles has come in, ²⁶ and in this way[e] all Israel will be saved. As it is written:

"The deliverer will come from Zion;
   he will turn godlessness away from Jacob.
²⁷ And this is[f] my covenant with them
   when I take away their sins."[g]

God's promise is that Israel shall come to Jesus and he will blot out their sins. That means all of Israel – Jews and Gentiles who have been grafted in shall be as one people.

Zechariah. 12: 10 "And I will pour out on the house of David and the inhabitants of Jerusalem a spirit[a] of grace and supplication. They will look on[b] me, the one they have pierced, and they will mourn for him as one mourns for an only child, and grieve bitterly for him as one grieves for a firstborn son. 11 On that day the weeping in Jerusalem will be as great as the weeping of Hadad Rimmon in the plain of Megiddo. 12 The land will mourn, each clan by itself, with their wives by themselves: the clan of the house of David and their wives, the clan of the house of Nathan and their wives, 13 the clan of the house of Levi and their wives, the clan of Shimei and their wives, 14 and all the rest of the clans and their wives.

Christ's Coming

At Christ's return to earth, he shall throw the devil in a pit for a thousand years. Because of it, there will be no evil on earth. Christ's millennial reign will cause many to receive Jesus because it will be like heaven on earth during those years. This period of Jesus on earth is known as the first resurrection – the saints will reign with Jesus on the earth.

Revelation 20:1 And I saw an angel coming down out of heaven, having the key to the Abyss and holding in his hand a great chain. ²He seized the dragon, that ancient serpent, who is the devil, or Satan, and bound him for a thousand years. ³He threw him into the Abyss, and locked and sealed it over him, to keep him from deceiving the nations anymore until the thousand years were ended. After that, he must be set free for a short time.

⁴I saw thrones on which were seated those who had been given authority to judge. And I saw the souls of those who had been beheaded because of their testimony about Jesus and because of the word of God. They[a] had not worshiped the beast or its image and had not received its mark on their foreheads or their hands. They came to life and reigned with Christ a thousand years. ⁵(The rest of the dead did not come to life until the thousand years were ended.) This is the first resurrection.⁶Blessed and holy are those who share in the first resurrection. The second death has no power over them, but they will be priests of God and of Christ and will reign with him for a thousand years.

After the thousand years of peace on earth, the devil will be released from the pit once more. Some people, although they lived in heaven on earth with Jesus ruling for the thousand years, will still choose to serve the devil. They will gather together all nations surrounding Israel to attack and destroy her. It will be the shortest war ever. God will come mightily and deliver Israel and defeat the enemy army forever. There will be much blood shed. The final judgement of the devil and his demons will occur. Those who chose to side with the devil against God will also share the same fate.

Revelation 20: [7] When the thousand years are over, Satan will be released from his prison [8] and will go out to deceive the nations in the four corners of the earth—Gog and Magog—and to gather them for battle. In number they are like the sand on the seashore. [9] They marched across the breadth of the earth and surrounded the camp of God's people, the city he loves. But fire came down from heaven and devoured them. [10] And the devil, who deceived them, was thrown into the lake of burning sulfur, where the beast and the false prophet had been thrown. They will be tormented day and night for ever and ever.

The description of the last war that ends all wars is describes in both the Old Covenant and the New Covenant. The place is in Armageddon. It will be the last war. It is the devil and his evil army against Jesus and his army of angels and saints. It will end the age as we know it on earth.

Rev 16: 16 Then they gathered the kings together to the place that in Hebrew is called Armageddon.

17 The seventh angel poured out his bowl into the air, and out of the temple came a loud voice from the throne, saying, "It is done!" 18 Then there came flashes of lightning, rumblings, peals of thunder and a severe earthquake. No earthquake like it has ever occurred since mankind has been on earth, so tremendous was the quake. 19 The great city split into three parts, and the cities of the nations collapsed. God remembered Babylon the Great and gave her the cup filled with the wine of the fury of his wrath.

Revelation 19: 11 I saw heaven standing open and there before me was a white horse, whose rider is called Faithful and True. With justice he judges and wages war. 12 His eyes are like blazing fire, and on his head are many crowns. He has a name written on him that no one knows but he himself. 13 He is dressed in a robe dipped in blood, and his name is the Word of God. 14 The armies of heaven were following him, riding on white horses and dressed in fine linen, white and clean. [15] Coming out of his mouth is a sharp sword with which to strike down the nations. "He will rule them with an iron scepter."[a] He treads the winepress of the fury of the wrath of God Almighty. [16] On his robe and on his thigh he has this name written:

KING OF KINGS AND LORD OF LORDS.

[17] And I saw an angel standing in the sun, who cried in a loud voice to all the birds flying in midair, "Come, gather together for the great supper of God, [18] so that you may eat the flesh of kings, generals, and the mighty, of horses and their riders, and the flesh of all people, free and slave, great and small."

[19] Then I saw the beast and the kings of the earth and their armies gathered together to wage war against the rider on the horse and his army. [20] But the beast was captured, and with it the false prophet who had performed the signs on its behalf. With these signs he had deluded those who had received the mark of the beast and worshiped its image. The two of them were thrown alive into the fiery lake of burning sulfur. [21] The rest were killed with the sword coming out of the mouth of the rider on the horse, and all the birds gorged themselves on their flesh.

In the book of Revelation prophecy – the devil – opposes Israel – and the final war will be over Israel. All surrounding nations will try to destroy Israel, but God will release angels and the army of God – saints and angels to defend Israel.

There are prophecies regarding this final war and the end of the earth as we know it. It is described in Ezekiel. The devil will quickly gather as many as will be used by him to fight against Israel and against Jesus and the saints. Amazingly, people will choose to fight against Jesus and against Israel after experiencing 1,000 years of peace and protection.

It will be a war with much violence and blood shed. There will be bodies lying all over the earth. It is also described in the Old Covenant in the books of Ezekiel and Daniel.

Ezekiel 38: 14"Therefore, son of man, prophesy and say to Gog: 'This is what the Sovereign LORD says: In that day, when my people Israel are living in safety, will you not take notice of it? 15You will come from your place in the far north, you and many nations with you, all of them riding on horses, a great horde, a mighty army. 16You will advance against my people Israel like a cloud that covers the land. In days to come, Gog, I will bring you against my land, so that the nations may know me when I am proved holy through you before their eyes.

[17] "'This is what the Sovereign LORD says: You are the one I spoke of in former days by my servants the prophets of Israel. At that time, they prophesied for years that I would bring you against them. [18] This is what will happen in that day: When Gog attacks the land of Israel, my hot anger will be aroused, declares the Sovereign LORD. [19] In my zeal and fiery wrath I declare that at that time there shall be a great earthquake in the land of Israel. [20] The fish in the sea, the birds in the sky, the beasts of the field, every creature that moves along the ground, and all the people on the face of the earth will tremble at my presence. The mountains will be overturned, the cliffs will crumble and every wall will fall to the ground. [21] I will summon a sword against Gog on all my mountains, declares the Sovereign LORD. Every man's sword will be against his brother. [22] I will execute judgment on him with plague and bloodshed; I will pour down torrents of rain, hailstones and burning sulfur on him and on his troops and on the many nations with him. [23] And so I will show my greatness and my holiness, and I will make myself known in the sight of many nations. Then they will know that I am the LORD.'

God's promise is that all of Israel shall return to God. There is promise for protection and blessing upon Israel even though all surrounding nations will gather together against her. The attack is not merely on the land of Israel but on God's covenant with Israel. God cherishes Israel and chooses to live there and reign from Jerusalem, during the millennium. Those who oppose and fight against Israel are directly fighting against God. This is the last war and it will end all wars. It will not be long, but it will be horrible.

Ezekiel 39: 7 "'I will make known my holy name among my people Israel. I will no longer let my holy name be profaned, and the nations will know that I the LORD am the Holy One in Israel. 8 It is coming! It will surely take place, declares the Sovereign LORD. This is the day I have spoken of.

9 "'Then those who live in the towns of Israel will go out and use the weapons for fuel and burn them up—the small and large shields, the bows and arrows, the war clubs and spears. For seven years they will use them for fuel. 10 They will not need to gather wood from the fields or cut it from the forests, because they will use the weapons for fuel. And they will plunder those who plundered them and loot those who looted them, declares the Sovereign LORD.

11 "'On that day I will give Gog a burial place in Israel, in the valley of those who travel east of the Sea. It will block the way of travelers, because Gog and all his hordes will be buried there. So it will be called the Valley of Hamon Gog.[b]

¹² "'For seven months the Israelites will be burying them in order to cleanse the land. ¹³ All the people of the land will bury them, and the day I display my glory will be a memorable day for them, declares the Sovereign LORD. ¹⁴ People will be continually employed in cleansing the land. They will spread out across the land and, along with others, they will bury any bodies that are lying on the ground.

"'After the seven months they will carry out a more detailed search. ¹⁵ As they go through the land, anyone who sees a human bone will leave a marker beside it until the gravediggers bury it in the Valley of Hamon Gog, ¹⁶ near a town called Hamonah.[c] And so they will cleanse the land.'

¹⁷ "Son of man, this is what the Sovereign LORD says: Call out to every kind of bird and all the wild animals: 'Assemble and come together from all around to the sacrifice I am preparing for you, the great sacrifice on the mountains of Israel. There you will eat flesh and drink blood. ¹⁸ You will eat the flesh of mighty men and drink the blood of the princes of the earth as if they were rams and lambs, goats and bulls—all of them fattened animals from Bashan. ¹⁹ At the sacrifice I am preparing for you, you will eat fat till you are glutted and drink blood till you are drunk. ²⁰ At my table you will eat your fill of horses and riders, mighty men and soldiers of every kind,' declares the Sovereign LORD.

²¹ "I will display my glory among the nations, and all the nations will see the punishment I inflict and the hand I lay on them. ²² From that day forward the people of Israel will know that I am the LORD their God. ²³ And the nations will know that the people of Israel went into exile for their sin, because they were unfaithful to me. So I hid my face from them and handed them over to their enemies, and they all fell by the sword. ²⁴ I dealt with them according to their uncleanness and their offenses, and I hid my face from them.

²⁵ "Therefore this is what the Sovereign LORD says: I will now restore the fortunes of Jacob[d] and will have compassion on all the people of Israel, and I will be zealous for my holy name. ²⁶ They will forget their shame and all the unfaithfulness they showed toward me when they lived in safety in their land with no one to make them afraid. ²⁷ When I have brought them back from the nations and have gathered them from the countries of their enemies, I will be proved holy through them in the sight of many nations. ²⁸ Then they will know that I am the LORD their God, for though I sent them into exile among the nations, I will gather them to their own land, not leaving any behind. ²⁹ I will no longer hide my face from them, for I will pour out my Spirit on the people of Israel, declares the Sovereign LORD."

This final war is also described by the multitude that no one can count who worship God and the lamb (Jesus). Israel will be completely wholly God's as Jesus reigns on the earth and He will defend Israel from any attacks against her. Miraculously, God will gather His army of saints, Jesus as King of Kings and Lord of Lords will lead. There is no place for the devil because Jesus has all authority because of his blood shed for us. The armies of God include all the angels and all the saints. It is God's Holy Spirit that is our champion. It is Jesus Holy blood shed for us that gives us victory. The glorious army of God will triumph as God executes judgement upon the devil and all that gather with him. It is the final judgement. God will cast the devil into an everlasting torment. There will be the end of evil, death, sickness, disease, suffering, was etc. The curse of sin is judged eternally. No longer will sin remain. There will be peace, prosperity, blessing and abundance in God's kingdom. All people will worship Jesus. All of Israel shall come to know Jesus the Messiah. All people will be living with God always. There will be a new heavens and earth.

Nations have opposed and tried to destroy Israel – repeatedly. Some succeeded in taking the land, the people captive – yet faith – God's covenant with Israel was there to protect her. There is always a remnant of God's people who serve, honour and live for him. The Hebrew language as been preserved even though Israelites were scattered throughout the earth. There are always those who believe in Judaism. The present-day Messianic Jews — are the first fruits of Israel coming back to God. They worship Jesus the Messiah as well as keep the Jewish festivals and traditions.

18 NEW HEAVENS AND EARTH: THE NEW JERUSALEM

The earth and universes as we know them today will remain as long as the "earth remains" (Genesis 8) but after the final war, God will create a new heaven and a new earth. It is somethings new. Surely it will be magnificent as it is described in scripture as a most beautiful place. The New Jerusalem will be our dwelling place. Our destiny is the New Jerusalem. God chose Israel. God chose Jerusalem as his dwelling place throughout the Scriptures. The New Jerusalem is to be the dwelling place for all believers. There will be no new temple there because God and the Lamb are the Temple. God dwells with us The Lamb (Jesus) is the light of it.

Revelation 21:1 Then I saw "a new heaven and a new earth,"[a] for the first heaven and the first earth had passed away, and there was no longer any sea. ²I saw the Holy City, the new Jerusalem, coming down out of heaven from God, prepared as a bride beautifully dressed for her husband. ³And I heard a loud voice from the throne saying, "Look! God's dwelling place is now among the people, and he will dwell with them. They will be his people, and God himself will be with them and be their God. ⁴'He will wipe every tear from their eyes. There will be no more death'[b] or mourning or crying or pain, for the old order of things has passed away."

⁵He who was seated on the throne said, "I am making everything new!" Then, he said, "Write this down, for these words are trustworthy and true."

⁶He said to me: "It is done. I am the Alpha and the Omega, the Beginning and the End. To the thirsty I will give water without cost from the spring of the water of life. ⁷Those who are victorious will inherit all this, and I will be their God and they will be my children. ⁸But the cowardly, the unbelieving, the vile, the murderers, the sexually immoral, those who practice magic arts, the idolaters and all liars—they will be consigned to the fiery lake of burning sulfur. This is the second death."

The foundations of the New Jerusalem are the 12 tribes of Israel and the 12 Apostles of the lamb. Our earthly history is most significant in the 12 tribes of Israel and the 12 Apostles of the lamb. They are the foundations for the New Jerusalem. The Holy Scriptures are essential in the building of it.

Revelation 21: ⁹One of the seven angels who had the seven bowls full of the seven last plagues came and said to me, "Come, I will show you the bride, the wife of the Lamb." ¹⁰And he carried me away in the Spirit to a mountain great and high, and showed me the Holy City, Jerusalem, coming down out of heaven from God. ¹¹It shone with the glory of God, and its brilliance was like that of a very precious jewel, like a jasper, clear as crystal. [12] It had a great, high wall with twelve gates, and with twelve angels at the gates. On the gates were written the names of the twelve tribes of Israel. [13] There were three gates on the east, three on the north, three on the south and three on the west. [14] The wall of the city had twelve foundations, and on them were the names of the twelve apostles of the Lamb.

[22] I did not see a temple in the city, because the Lord God Almighty and the Lamb are its temple. [23] The city does not need the sun or the moon to shine on it, for the glory of God gives it light, and the Lamb is its lamp. [24] The nations will walk by its light, and the kings of the earth will bring their splendor into it. [25] On no day will its gates ever be shut, for there will be no night there. [26] The glory and honor of the nations will be brought into it. [27] Nothing impure will ever enter it, nor will anyone who does what is shameful or deceitful, but only those whose names are written in the Lamb's book of life.

The glory of the nations of the earth will bring their glory to the New Jerusalem – all nations, ethnicities. There will be lush gardens of beauty and fruit, The New Jerusalem is described as a most desirable place to live. It is a glorious beautiful destiny. It is more than the Garden of Eden restored. It is life beyond what we have ever known because we will be in God's Holy presence eternally.

Revelation 22 Then the angel showed me the river of the water of life, as clear as crystal, flowing from the throne of God and of the Lamb 2 down the middle of the great street of the city. On each side of the river stood the tree of life, bearing twelve crops of fruit, yielding its fruit every month. And the leaves of the tree are for the healing of the nations. 3 No longer will there be any curse. The throne of God and of the Lamb will be in the city, and his servants will serve him. 4 They will see his face, and his name will be on their foreheads. 5 There will be no more night. They will not need the light of a lamp or the light of the sun, for the Lord God will give them light. And they will reign for ever and ever.

Conclusion

This book highlights key aspects of Israel's Scriptural history that apply to both Jews and Christians. It is essential that Christians realize that we share a destiny with Jewish people – with Israel. Not only do we share it, but we are part of it because Jesus Christ the Messiah made the way possible. Many Christians understand that Jesus is God. Many Christians do not know that Messiah Jesus is for both Christians and Jews and that Israel is in the heart of God. God keeps His covenants. He made covenant with Abraham, Isaac, Jacob. He made covenant with Moses. Through the blood of Jesus Christ, we inherit the blessings of the covenant of Israel. We have been grafted into Israel through Jesus Christ. By the same mercy or grace that saved us, Israel shall once more be grafted in and we will be one people. Our destiny is the New Jerusalem.

It should compel us as Christians to pray for Israel and for Jewish people. Praying for Israel is praying for God's people. Pray for the peace and protection of the nation as well as the people because God's covenant is with Israel. God always keeps His covenant. He blesses those who bless Israel and fights against those who fight against Israel.

Ps 122: **Pray for the peace of Jerusalem: "May those who love you be secure.**

⁷May there be peace within your walls
  and security within your citadels."
⁸For the sake of my family and friends,
  I will say, "Peace be within you."
⁹For the sake of the house of the LORD our God,
  I will seek your prosperity.

In these chapters, I have pointed to God's relationship starting with Israel so that we could agree, God first chose Israel to be His people. He revealed himself through his covenants with Israel: Adam, Abraham, Isaac, Jacob, David, Moses: Jesus Christ.

Our heritage as Christians is shared with Israel only because of Jesus Christ. Through Jesus Christ, we are cleansed and made one with God. Israel was the plan of God from the start. The 12 tribes of Israel are the foundations of the Israel people. The 12 Apostles of the lamb are the foundations of Jesus Christ's Church. Both are together. You cannot separate them. We were made joint heirs with Jesus. The blessings of the covenants God made with Israel are ours by faith in Jesus. Our destiny is with Israel. We will both dwell together as one people with Jesus the Messiah. Our heritage is the land of Israel and Jerusalem. Our destiny is the New Jerusalem.

Practical Application points

Take a stand for Israel with words, choices, finances and volunteerism Never allow Jewish people to be mistreated. Have no tolerance for prejudice.

Purchase Israeli. Support Israel by sowing into the people. There are many businesses and organizations world renown. Do the opposite of those who hate Israel – build up Israel with words, with finances with positive actions. Judaica is a marketplace for Israeli goods of all types. I highly recommend them as a reputable excellent business.

Messianic worship and praise

There are multitudes of talented beautiful Messianic and praise musicians and psalmists.

Galilea of the Nations is an excellent Messianic Christian company known for its praise and worship.

Messianic celebrations of Jewish festivals

The Messianic Jewish celebration of the festivals is worth being a part of. Although not necessary, it is worthwhile because Christ is described in them. Should you get a chance to celebrate these with a Messianic congregation, please do. Robin Samson has an excellent book on the Jewish feasts that explain the Jewish festivals and include craft templates for children. Jews for Jesus has materials on the feasts and the truths of Jesus as Messiah.

Honour Israel. It is our heritage. Our destinies are shared.

Pray for Israel.

Align with Messianic Christian churches.

Strongly align with Jews against any type of antisemitism. John Hagee and Christians United for Israel honour Israel and host events to honour Israel and promote Israeli Christian friendship.

Never forget WWII what was done to over 6 million Jews.

Teach truths of Israel as God's people.

Teach all the scripture not only the New Covenant.

Promote Christian Tourism to Israel

Epilogue

The New Jerusalem our destiny.

Those written in the Lamb's Book of life are those redeemed by Jesus the Messiah.

Revelation 21: [22] I did not see a temple in the city, because the Lord God Almighty and the Lamb are its temple. [23] The city does not need the sun or the moon to shine on it, for the glory of God gives it light, and the Lamb is its lamp. [24] The nations will walk by its light, and the kings of the earth will bring their splendor into it. [25] On no day will its gates ever be shut, for there will be no night there. [26] The glory and honor of the nations will be brought into it. [27] Nothing impure will ever enter it, nor will anyone who does what is shameful or deceitful, but only those whose names are written in the Lamb's book of life.

Pray that the preaching of the gospel will reach all nations and all ethnicities and peoples of the earth. Pray for the Holy Spirit to move in revival on the earth so that the Church wants Christ to come. It is prophesied He will come only when these two things occur. The gospel must reach all people of the earth. They must get the chance to receive Christ once. The Church who is yearning for Jesus to return will not be trying to escape the earth but rather see Jesus come as ruler of the earth. As the Church is inspired by the Holy Spirit, she prays "Come Lord Jesus". As the Holy Spirit and the Church are together, Jesus shall come.

Revelation 22: [12] "Look, I am coming soon! My reward is with me, and I will give to each person according to what they have done. [13] I am the Alpha and the Omega, the First and the Last, the Beginning and the End.

[14] "Blessed are those who wash their robes, that they may have the right to the tree of life and may go through the gates into the city. [15] Outside are the dogs, those who practice magic arts, the sexually immoral, the murderers, the idolaters and everyone who loves and practices falsehood.

[16] "I, Jesus, have sent my angel to give you[a] this testimony for the churches. I am the Root and the Offspring of David, and the bright Morning Star."

[17] The Spirit and the bride say, "Come!" And let the one who hears say, "Come!" Let the one who is thirsty come; and let the one who wishes take the free gift of the water of life.

Reflection questions

1. Explain the dual nature of Israel (use at least 3 examples) and the results of it.
2. Compare dual nature to modern Christian life.
3. Explain God's covenant with Abraham. What did it include?
4. Explain how the covenant of Abraham applies to us as Christians.
5. Explain God's covenant with Moses. What did it include?
6. Explain how the Mosaic covenant applies to our lives as Christians.
7. Discuss (3 points or more) the significance of God's presence with His people a shown throughout the book. (God's Spirit on prophets, God's presence in the Tabernacle, God's presence in the Temple, God's presence in Christian lives.)
8. Explain why the destiny of Christians is connected to Israel.
9. List some things you've considered or learned because of the book especially the scriptures.
10. What ways can you personally make a difference to Israel? List some things you can do to align yourself with Israel.

PRAYERS

PRAYERS

The following prayers are samples of prayers you could pray for important reasons. You could pray the same meaning in your own words. The prayers are meant as examples only.

PRAYER FOR SALVATION

Thank you- Jesus that you died for me on the cross. Thank you that you rose from the dead and ascended into heaven. Thank you that you are coming back again. I thank you Jesus for forgiving my sins. Thank you for your blood that cleanses me from all sin and unrighteousness. Thank you that your blood makes me holy. Thank you for saving me. Fill me with the Holy Spirit to overflowing. I pray for the baptism of the Holy Spirit. Lead me to other people who love you and serve you and that can help me know more about you. Give me the discerning of spirits strong. I thank you and praise you. With my mouth, I confess Jesus Christ is my LORD. Amen.

PRAYER FOR BAPTISM OF THE HOLY SPIRIT

Thank you- Jesus that you promised to send the gift of the Holy Spirit to us. Thank you that this promise is to all believers. I am a believer. I want all of you that you will give me. I want to know you God. Baptize me in the Holy Spirit with the evidence of speaking in other tongues. I believe you want to fill me to overflowing with your Spirit so that I might be an effective witness for Christ on the earth. Thank you for saving me. Thank you for your Holy presence. [begin praising God for what He has done for you – sing worship choruses and praise God in your natural language. Believe that He is present with you – start praising and worshipping Him. As phrases come to you in other tongues, say them – praise God with new tongues.] I praise you. I thank you. I receive the baptism of the Holy Spirit.

PRAYER FOR RELEASING ANGELS

God, I thank you that angels are ministering spirits sent as ministers to us. I pray over my prayer request NAME IT HERE. God I pray release angels to perform it. I thank you for releasing the answer to me. I praise you for it. Amen.

PRAYER FOR RESISTING EVIL

I am the redeemed of the LORD. Jesus Christ has saved me. I am a new creation in Christ Jesus. Jesus blood covers me. I live in the spirit. The Holy Spirit of God fills my spirit. O Holy Spirit quicken me; give me wisdom. Pray [expecting God will give you discerning of spirits so you will have the right words to speak.]

In the name of Jesus Christ, I bind you. I rebuke you evil spirit. In the name of Jesus, I command you to go out. You have no place in my life. I cast you out. You have no place with me. I am covered by the blood of Jesus and His righteousness is my righteousness. Go out evil spirit in the name of Jesus Christ!

Thank you, Holy Spirit for your holy presence. Release angels to drive out the enemy. Thank you. Amen.

PRAYER FOR PROTECTION

Holy Spirit release angels to protect me. I plead the blood of Jesus over me. I pray the protection you promise to your people. Cover me Jesus. Holy Spirit give me wisdom, discernment and understanding. Thank you for angels that guard over me. Thank you for your blood that protects me and a hedge of protection around me. I praise you O God. [praise God with some worship choruses and expect God's holy presence to be manifest in you]. Thank you. O God for protection.

PRAYER FOR HEALING

Lord Jesus, thank you that you gave your life for me so that I can be saved, healed and delivered. I thank you for the scripture that by your stripes I am healed. I thank you for my healing.

NAME THE DISEASE I bind you in the name of Jesus. I cast you out. I pray over myself that I would be whole spirit, soul and body.

Thank you, God. for your healing manifestation in my life. I give you all the glory. Amen.

PRAYER OF REPENTENCE

Jesus, thank you for your blood shed for me. I repent of the sin of NAME IT. I thank you for liberty from sin. I cut off the root of iniquity in my family. I thank you for your empowering presence to live a Holy life. Holy Spirit lead and guide me in the paths of righteousness. Thank you for giving me godly desires. Let my life align with your word. In Jesus name. Amen.

Prayer of dedication as a giver

God, thank you for prospering me. Let me be a giver you can use to give to others. God let my character be humble and giving so that you place things and wealth in my hands, and I will give as you lead me. If you prosper me with more than enough, I will obey your promptings to give to the gospel, to people and for the glory of God. Use me as a giver. I give myself wholly to you. In Jesus name. Amen.

Prayer for Israel

God I pray for the peace of Jerusalem (Psalm 122: 6). I pray for all of Israel to be saved (Romans 11: 25). I pray for you to make Jerusalem a praise and a fame throughout all the earth. (Isaiah 62:7). I pray you will keep Israel as the apple of your eye and hide her under

the shadow of your wing. (Psalm 17:8). I pray for the Word of God to be written in their hearts.
(Jeremiah 31: 33; Ezekiel 11: 19) Reveal yourself as Jesus the Messiah to the people of Israel and Jewish people everywhere.
Amen.

Of course, you can pray other things for the blessing of Israel. It is essential to pray scripture as God has made covenant with Israel.

OTHER BOOKS BY CHRIS A. LEGEBOW

Available on Amazon.ca Amazon.com or Kindle

By Living Word Publishers

Angels: Ministering Spirits

Discipling the Generation

An Excellent Spirit: Living Life Wholly Unto God

Covenant With God: God's Relationship With Man

Discovering and Using your Spiritual Gifts

Discipling The Generation

Divine Healing in the Scriptures: God's Mercy Towards Man

Jesus Christ: Saviour, Healer, Deliverer, LORD

Kinds of Giving: From the Holy Scriptures

Signs of Jesus Coming

OTHER BOOKS BY
CHRIS A. LEGEBOW Continued...

Spheres of Authority: Know yours

The Commandments

The Doctrine of Christ: Essential Truths of Scripture

The Five-Fold Ministry: Gifts to the Church

Kinds of Prayer. Knowing Them and Using Them Effectively

Living Life Fully: Knowing your Purpose

The Anointing: The Glory of God

The Charismatic Christian Church

The High Calling: Life Worth Living

The High Life: Communion with the Holy Spirit

The Sacraments: A Charismatic Guide

ABOUT THE AUTHOR

Chris Legebow is a Christian Professor of English and Communications. She has taught at the elementary, high school and College and University levels. She has ministered in her local churches in intercessory prayer, teaching Sunday school and other Christian Doctrine classes to children and youth. She has preached to congregations and given her testimony. Although she was not raised in a Christian home, she came to know Jesus Christ as her Saviour and LORD while she was studying in University. This radically transformed her life in terms of priorities and commitment.

She has a strong passion for the great commission – that Jesus Christ would be preached throughout all the earth believing that it a major sign of the LORD's return. She has been a part of several different types of full gospel charismatic churches but has also gained much of her insight and enlightenment from Christian Media and broadcasting. She hopes to continue ministering, serving, interceding and giving and teaching until the LORD returns.

www.ingramcontent.com/pod-product-compliance
Lightning Source LLC
Chambersburg PA
CBHW031443040426
42444CB00007B/954